FORMAL METHODS AND EMPIRICAL PRACTICES

CSLI Lecture Notes Number 205

FORMAL METHODS
AND
EMPIRICAL PRACTICES

Conversations with Patrick Suppes

Foreword by
Patrick Suppes

Roberta Ferrario & Viola Schiaffonati

CSLI
PUBLICATIONS
*Center for the Study of
Language and Information
Stanford, California*

Copyright © 2012
CSLI Publications
Center for the Study of Language and Information
Leland Stanford Junior University
Printed in the United States
16 15 14 13 12   1 2 3 4 5

Library of Congress Cataloging-in-Publication Data

Ferrario, Roberta.
Formal methods and empirical practices : conversations with
Patrick Suppes / Roberta Ferrario, Viola Schiaffonati.
    p. cm.
(CSLI lecture notes ; no. 205)
Includes bibliographical references and index.
ISBN 978-1-57586-651-2 (cloth : alk. paper) –
ISBN 978-1-57586-652-9 (pbk. : alk. paper)
ISBN 978-1-57586-650-5 (electronic)
1. Science–Methodology. 2. Science–Philosophy. 3. Suppes, Patrick,
1922–Interviews. 4. Philosophers–United States–Interviews.
5. Scientists–United States–Interviews. I. Schiaffonati, Viola.
II. Center for the Study of Language and Information (U.S.)
III. Title.

Q175.3.F47 2012

                                                         500–dc23
                        CIP

CSLI Publications gratefully acknowledges a generous gift from
Jill and Donald Knuth in support of scholarly publishing
that has made the production of this book possible.

CSLI was founded in 1983 by researchers from Stanford University, SRI
International, and Xerox PARC to further the research and development of
integrated theories of language, information, and computation. CSLI headquarters
and CSLI Publications are located on the campus of Stanford University.

CSLI Publications reports new developments in the study of language,
information, and computation. Please visit our web site at
http://cslipublications.stanford.edu/
for comments on this and other titles, as well as for changes
and corrections by the author and publisher.

Contents

Foreword

One of the pleasures of being around long enough to be thought of as senior is to talk to younger philosophers. This book started as a series of conversations between Roberta Ferrario, Viola Schiaffonati, and me, and we decided to record them. Like almost all such recordings, ours were a long way from being publishable. Roberta and Viola have taken over and created something coherent. I have enjoyed reading their efforts. They make my favorite topics in the philosophy of science more accessible to philosophers and others who would like to have a broad overview of the foundations of science, without all the rather onerous technical details.

I hope many persons will enjoy reading what they have to say about axiomatization, representation and invariance of scientific structures, and how these ideas of formalization can be applied to experiments, particularly for the probabilistic structure of most experimental data. They have expressed well my claim that the analysis of experiments is philosophically just as important as the analysis of theories.

I also want to comment on the individual chapters. The first one is concerned with central debates in the philosophy of science, about which I have taken positions, but sometimes in an implicit form.

In Chapter 2, Roberta and Viola examine in detail, with a step-by-step analysis, the methodology of my formal approach to the philosophy of science. Reading this reminds me of my own first effort to do this in an elementary way while writing, in 1957, the final chapter of my Introduction to Logic. Fortunately, they add something useful to that early discussion, and ones that followed, by being concerned with stating clearly what are the advantages of using this formal methodology. Among other things, they describe well my stress on the importance of moving from treating exactly verbal formulations of scientific laws, as the fundamental step, to the formulation of models. Closely related to this is my stress on finding canonical representations of models, as in the case of empirical structures in measurements being represented by numerical structures. (Note that I tend to use the terms structure and model interchangeably.) The next step is one often neglected by philosophers of science. This is the study of the invariance of the representations of an empirical structure. For example, consider the numerical structures representing the measurement of length, or, to put the matter more explicitly, the empirical structures for measuring length. These numerical structures are invariant up to multiplication by a positive constant, which corresponds, for example, to converting measurements from feet to meters. Although there is a good history of invariance being studied in group theory in pure mathematics in the 19th century, there are almost no papers on invariance in physics until the 20th century, the most famous, almost surely, being Einsteins 1905 paper on special relativity, which is actually entitled (in German, but given in English here), On the Electrodynamics of Moving Bodies.

In Chapter 3, Roberta and Viola compare my analysis of scientific theories to the one adopted by Carnap and others of the Vienna circle. This view, of course, has already been mentioned above implicitly, for it was Carnaps natural tendency to want to give a logical (and therefore verbal) rather than a set-theoretical mathematical analysis in terms of models. They also enter into the more subtle comparison of my views to those of structuralism, and also the related semantic view of theories. I will not try to enter into these details here, but I do like a summary that is often made in support of my approach. This is the slogan that mathematics is more useful in science by far than metamathematics, which was Tarskis baptism of logical studies of the structure of mathematical theories, such as proving whether a mathematical theory in a given formulation is complete or not. (I believe it was Tarski who first used this term metamathematics, but I could be wrong.)

In Chapter 4, Roberta and Viola comment extensively on my use of the concepts of structure and isomorphism of structures, which I remarked on briefly already. My own feeling for the centrality of these concepts in mathematics and science, and therefore, in the philosophy of science, has continued to increase. Perhaps the most important influence has been my rereading of Aristotles De Anima. The essential way he makes the perception of a physical object depend on the form of that object being received by the senses is to my mind one of the most original ideas of ancient Greek thought. The insight about the sameness of forms, e.g., the isomorphism between the shape of the signet ring and the shape that is in the mind (or as I would now say, in the brain), is, to my knowledge, not found in any other ancient culture. Indeed, it has only come to be fully appreciated in modern psychology and neuroscience with a focus on retinotopic maps in the visual cortex.

In Chapter 5, the final one, Roberta and Viola discuss more recent ideas of mine, even though some of them are ones I have been thinking about for a long time. A good example is the theory of errors in measurement, a subject already made prominent in the 18th century by Simpson and Laplace. In my mind, systematic treatment of this topic is by far the most important omission in the three-volume treatise Foundations of Measurement I wrote with David Krantz, Duncan Luce and Amos Tversky. We actually had a draft of a fairly long chapter on this topic, but we were not satisfied with it. More recently, I have written some particular things about inexact measurement, but this is clearly a subject I still have hopes of returning to. In some ways, this connects with my ideas about causality and spontaneity, which keep changing as well. Perhaps this is a good stopping point, appropriate as it is for underscoring how much is still left to be done on almost all the important questions in the philosophy of science.

26 February 2012

Patrick Suppes
Stanford, California

Preface

In January 2001 one of the authors of this book was introduced to Patrick Suppes by Claudia Arrighi, who at the time was a visiting scholar at the Center for the Study of Language and Information working on the Educational Program for the Gifted Youth project headed by Suppes. The meeting took place immediately after a memorial held in honor of Quine on the campus of Stanford University. The conversation that followed the introduction revolved mostly around the papers that were presented at the memorial. During this exchange, when discussing the papers, Suppes would invariably use the word "detailed" when critiquing them.

He praised some of the presentations given that day for the amount of detail they included while criticizing some of the other papers for their lack thereof. When we noticed the recurrent use of the word *detailed* in our conversation, we were pleasantly amused and we lightly proposed that the word can be used as standard to distinguish radically different ways of doing philosophy.

"Detail" may also be seen as the word that launched the present work and eventually becoming the thread that runs through it. Work on it began in the summer of 2002 after a series of exchanges with Suppes about his recently published *Representation and Invariance of Scientific Structures* (Suppes 2002).

We then proposed to Suppes to work on a manuscript based mostly on discussions with him about some central topics of his philosophy of science.

In preparation for our interviews, we read and studied *Representation and Invariance*. Though we did expect the book to reflect Suppes' attitude towards "details", we were pleasantly impressed by the extraordinary amount of "details" found in his 2002 book. This for us was quite unusual and surprising for a book of philosophy. We also thought that this amount of "details" could intimidate a beginning student in philosophy, and discourage her to read the book, thus depriving her from the opportunity to get to the important messages behind all the details. This was our main motivation for pursuing the interviews with him. We were also fortunate to have one of us spend the whole academic year 2003/2004 as a visiting scholar at CSLI working with Suppes.

This prolonged stay allowed for frequent informal and formal discussions with Suppes on some central philosophical points in a language accessible to a general philosophical readership while maintaining the richness of details and examples so typical of his approach.

At the beginning we thought of a book mainly consisting of these interviews but we decided that the book can benefit from our analysis and reflections on Suppes' work.

So this material, collected over a period of about seven years, constitutes the core of the book, together of course with the immense bibliography produced by Suppes in more than five decades of intense work. It is fair to say that these interviews are, in most cases, conversations. We started our sessions with a list of questions, that we soon realized we had to go beyond as new ideas and issues suggested more questions. Most of the recorded material we transcribed and revised with Suppes himself, giving birth to other reflections and conversations. If at the beginning the aim of our questions was primarily explanatory, then it has become more general, as we have understood that the best way to interact was not to pose specific questions to Suppes, but rather to propose general themes on which he was free to comment to his liking.

It is worth noting that some material the interviews are based on (in particular that present in Chapter 5) constitutes the latest results of Suppes' deep reflection on the subject of representation of science and is still mostly unpublished; this is the reason why often in that chapter we have included long quotations, in order to keep the original flavor of these novel ideas in Suppes' production. We had to make many editorial choices and, even if this book is strongly based on materials coming from our own personal interviews and conversations with Suppes, we the authors of the present volume are ultimately responsible for its contents.

We would like to thank the following people who helped make this project possible: first of all, Patrick Suppes, who has believed in the contribution to philosophy the project could bring and has dedicated his precious time to our interviews and to reading them afterwards; Dikran Karagueuzian, for his support and suggestions to re-direct our efforts to more fruitful ends and doing this with his proverbial witticisms; Maria Carla Galavotti, who has generously shared with us her competence on Suppes' philosophy; Charlotte Cattivera, for her practical support. Finally, we would like to thank Claudia Arrighi, who often joined us in our sessions with Suppes and often played the role of *trait d'union* between us and our American referents, but most of all, we thank her for her friendship that made our frequent trips to Palo Alto so pleasant and enjoyable.

1

Introduction

The central theme of this book is the relationship between formal methods and empirical practice in the representation of science. In this book we discuss some concepts, proposed and used by Patrick Suppes, in order to evaluate their methodological relevance in the scenario of the philosophical analysis of science, and in particular of scientific theories and experiments. So this book does not aim at presenting in a systematic and complete way all Suppes' philosophical production. Our main goal, rather, is to evaluate the methodological relevance of some ideas, such as the use of set theoretical models, of formalization, of models of data, of a theory of experiments, all within the scenario of a completely new vision of science and philosophy of science. We start by presenting Suppes' formal framework for the representation of scientific theories in terms of models, while investigating the sense and limits of this formalization, to finish with the analysis of the relationship between formal methods and empirical practice, with particular attention to the role played by experiments.

The direct use of formal methods in the philosophy of science and the intertwining of formal and empirically based methods are in our reading the two main distinguishing factors of Suppes' contribution, both to science and to philosophy. On the other hand, the path followed in the book also reflects the historical development of Suppes' shifts in the focus of interest. This, far from being univocally determined, as Suppes has always been completely open to stimuli coming from very different lines of research, has been mainly centered on formal and logical approaches in the old days, followed by his big investment in probabilistic studies, has then lately been very much oriented

1

toward empiricism, where again Suppes has been able to convey a novel and original perspective.

1.1 Philosopher of the details

The mix between philosophical insights and scientific results constitutes probably the most original trait of Suppes' work. It is not by chance that *Scientific Philosopher* is the title of a three volumes collection edited by Paul Humphreys (1994) presenting various articles dealing with the huge amount of subject matters that Suppes has explored in his long and fruitful career. Scientific philosopher, indeed, is the profile that emerges by looking at all the works done by Suppes and that he himself recognizes as representative of his attitude. Suppes has always supported the idea that a philosopher of science needs to know the details of scientific disciplines and this is in fact necessary if one wants to do the kind of philosophy of science he proposes. In order to be able to single out the primitive notions of a scientific discipline and to represent how they are related in a formal and axiomatic way, the philosopher of science needs to have come in close contact with the subject matter of that discipline. And disciplines must be studied in every aspect, starting from the gathering of data, their analysis, and the formulation of the theoretical part.

> I primarily thought of myself as a philosopher of science. I think this is probably not really the most accurate characterization. I continue to do and continue to have great interest in the philosophy of science, but it is certainly also true that, in many respects, more of my energy in the last quarter of a century has been devoted to scientific activities. [...] a distinction between philosophy of science and science is in itself incorrect. (Suppes 2006, 32)

Starting from the study of the foundations of sciences, Suppes has also given in some cases original contributions to the sciences themselves. In particular, in the psychology of learning, especially computer-aided learning, he has been a pioneer and an active researcher 'in the field'. Moreover, he has contributed in many respects in the field of the foundations of quantum mechanics, where he has been a widely recognized theoretician. Suppes thus has broken the boundaries of the competencies usually assigned to the philosopher of science, those of the context of the justification, to step into the context of discovery, normally territory of scientists only.

We believe that, besides the insightful characterization of scientific philosopher advanced by Humphreys, *philosopher of the details* can give reason as well for his attitude both toward philosophy and scientific research. Details in this context must be intended not as something inessential or superfluous, but as the sign of a deep and extended knowledge of a given subject matter. As the reader will soon recognize while reading this book, Suppes' *detailed* formal project in the philosophy of science constitutes the framework of our reflections and of our conversations. This is, of course, not the only perspective we wish to emphasize in a book that tries to systematically present some of Suppes' philosophical ideas, but it is certainly the one adopted to organize the whole material, a *fil rouge* in analyzing Suppes' production, apparently so diverse and heterogeneous.

The attention to details and the formal framework are in accord also with his more recent research on brain and its representations. This research does not constitute a chapter by itself in this book, as it consists in an ongoing work, but it is well represented in many interviews, especially those reported in the last chapter.

When we have started to think about this book, Suppes' formal approach to the philosophy of science has emerged as central in giving back a completely new vision of scientific theories. Suppes has been one of the first, if not the first one, to bring philosophy of science closer to the standards of rigor of scientific disciplines, while avoiding the rigidity of the former neopositivistic view. However, to exhaust Suppes' philosophy in a formal philosophy would be reductive; actually the attention to the formal is always mitigated in Suppes with the attention to experimentation (not a very common stance amongst philosophers of science), which manifests the limits of a formal treatment, accompanied with the attention to details together with a pluralist view of science. It is exactly this complex, but highly integrated, vision that makes Suppes' philosophy unique.

We have organized the following of this introduction under different headings for reasons of clarity: formal methods, pragmatism, pluralism and antireductionism. However, we do not think that the following lines are really separate in Suppes' research. We deem that these different elements are perfectly integrated in Suppes' philosophy of science, thus contributing to make him a fundamental actor within the whole scenario of the past, current, and future philosophy of science.

In the first part of the 2002 book (Suppes 2002) three elements are recognized as central by Suppes himself: formal methods, identified with set-theoretical methods, empirical details—intended as set-theoretical representation of data, historical background—conceived as analysis of the origins of concepts and theories. Let's start with the first one.

1.2   Formal methods

One of the goals of this book is to present Suppes' formal approach to philosophy, its method, range of application, problems, and limits, without being too technical but, at the same time, maintaining the attention to details that, as we have said before, are at the center of Suppes' philosophical enterprise.

It is Suppes' deep conviction that scientific theories may be analyzed using formal methods. By adopting formal methods the analysis becomes more precise, taking into account important details that can be lost at the general level of discourse. According to this view, formal methods constitute a general framework to systematically discuss important issues of the philosophy of science. These formal methods are identified by Suppes with set-theoretical methods, rather than with those of first-order logic, for a number of reasons which basically have to do with their power in expressing any systematic results of empirical sciences. Accordingly, the axiomatization of theories is carried out in terms of set-theoretical models, instead of as a purely logical calculus, with the aim to give back a representation of scientific theories closer to the actual practice and far from the standard and simplified sketch proposed by the neopositivistic view. In Suppes' words: "the axiomatization of a scientific theory within set theory is an important initial step in making its structure both exact and explicit" (Suppes 2002, 10). Set-theoretical structures provide the right setting for investigating problems of representation and invariance in any systematic part of science.

Suppes was initially drawn to formal methods during his early training in mathematics and, then, as an undergraduate at the University of Chicago. However, it was as a graduate student at Columbia University, as Ernest Nagel's student, that the acquaintance with formal methods became wider and applied to real problems.

> I was challenged and fascinated by the attempt to give rigorous physical foundations, rigorous in the physical sense that is, but still formal in the sense of ending up with the standard differential equations. (Suppes 2005, 138)

The final step in this process of acquaintance to formal methods, in particular on how to do formal research, was when Suppes moved to Stanford in 1950 as young instructor under the tutelage of McKinsey, with whom he wrote his first works and who suggested him the attendance of Tarski's graduate seminar at Berkeley:

> Watching Tarski at work was a lesson of the greatest value in appreciating and understanding at a deeper level what could be accomplished with the highest standards of intellectual clarity. (Suppes 2005, 139)

But what is the role of formal methods in philosophy, and in philosophy of science in particular? The first answer is that they provide a foundation for mathematics and for the sciences. More precisely, formal methods can be used to clarify the foundations of the specific parts of different branches of science, such as the foundations of the theory of measurement (Scott and Suppes 1958), or the foundations of stochastic models of learning in psychology (Suppes 1969), both fields in which Suppes has offered a central contribution. And what does it mean to give philosophical foundations of scientific disciplines? It means to clarify the basic notions and concepts at the roots of a discipline. This does not imply that philosophers study the philosophy of physics, for instance, by doing something different from what physicists do. It is rather that philosophers tend to concentrate, both by taste and by training, on foundational questions.

> So, when asked about the relation of philosophy to other disciplines, my answer is now, and has been in the past, that philosophers are concerned with foundations. They are concerned with concentrating on the concepts that are fundamental to a given discipline whether it be mathematics, physics, economics, or psychology. The methods they use for these investigations are pretty much the same methods in broad terms that are used by the scientists working in a given discipline. They just use these methods to apply a very focused analysis on the foundations, and of course, it is also correct to emphasize that in many cases they bring to such study concepts used in another discipline but ordinarily not concepts that have been developed only by philosophers. (Suppes 2005, 147)

What emerges is that Suppes does not believe in a strict separation between philosophy of science and science. It is more a matter of interest and attitude the fact that philosophers are attracted by foundational questions, while physicists most of the times do not consider them, even though we cannot exclud *a priori* that some of them show some interest, as it is clear by looking at the history of science.

> [...] a distinction between philosophy of science and science is in itself incorrect. In many ways I am sympathetic with such a summary of Quine's view, namely, that philosophy should mainly itself be science. This is a way of saying that philosophy is not privy to any special methods different from the methods used in the sciences. I certainly much agree with these ideas, but also that there are special aspects of problems that are of particular philosophical interest and often cultivated only by philosophers. Current philosophers of physics do not expect to develop purely philosophical theories of space and time, but rather, make philosophical commentaries on the work done by physicists. (Suppes 2006, 32)

This is also the reason why we have to be very careful in evaluating the role of formal methods in science. Actually, from the one side, they constitute a sort of *lingua franca* of pure mathematics and they can play a very useful role in representing scientific theories. On the other side, scientists themselves do not very often use such languages, since basically they do not do mathematics and, thus, they adopt a more informal approach.

However, even if good arguments are used both by philosophers and scientists, one thing that philosophers are particularly interested in is to analyze the methodological issues, such as what kinds of arguments or what kinds of evidence are used:"[...] so I think the concern with justification, evidence, and argument are particular features of philosophy" (Frauchinger 2008, 166). This does not mean that a physicist does not need to understand how to use arguments and evidence, but that probably his or her method and attitude would be different from that of a philosopher.

In characterizing Suppes' formal methods, it is important to acknowledge that he has been deeply influenced by his own work as experimental scientist and this aspect is the reason of the central importance he ascribes to experimentation (Galavotti 1994). The famous paper "Models of data" (Suppes 1962) represents the first systematic effort to use formal methods on the problems of data. This paper shows very well how difficult it is to abstract from the details of experiments to give a set-theoretical characterization of data. In a sense, experimental details are endless and Suppes emphasizes the necessity of abstracting from data, a theme which he has continually returned to (Suppes 2005).

Suppes' work in the foundations of the theory of measurement represents very well his attention to formal methods connected to empirical details, and his attempt to give of them a set-theoretical characterization as well. In Suppes' words, the theory combines a demand for correct and formal results with the continual analysis typical of experimental procedures in a variety of sciences (Suppes 1979b).

The attention to experimentation is the key to understand the limits of the formal approach, also the one conducted in terms of set-theoretical methods advocated by Suppes, which can be more precise than the logical one in representing scientific theories, but that cannot be exhaustive.

> It is only a myth engendered by philosophers—even in the past to some extent by myself—that the deductive organization of physics in nice set-theoretical form is an achievable goal. A look at the chaos in the current literature in any part of physics is enough to quickly dispel that illusion. This does not mean that set-theoretical work cannot be done, it is just that its severe limitations must be recognized. (Suppes 1994, 214)

Besides the limitations of set-theoretical methods in science, also those in the philosophy of science must be recognized. Actually, foundational studies, in which formal methods can be adopted, are not the whole of philosophy of science, though probably a major part. For example, the study of experiments, certainly a fundamental part of philosophy of science, cannot be done in formal terms, as a set-theoretical formulation of how to make an experiment is not possible. On the contrary, the study of experiments must be focussed more on *apprenticeship*, and practice should be emphasized in the context of experimentation:

> [...] the way to becoming a competent experimenter is usually by being an apprentice to somebody who knows more than you do and has been doing it for a long time, who is familiar with the equipment and with the experiment. It's one of the roles of being a graduate student, for example, in advanced sciences: learning how to do experiments. (Interview, 1 April 2009)

Practice, apprenticeship, and the way in which experiments are really carried out in the single scientific disciplines seem to cover a central role in Suppes' current interests. This is not to be read in contraposition with his initial interest in axiomatization and formal methods, but rather as a refinement and completion of it. The aim, thus, is to build mathematical structures that more closely match scientific practice, making the theoretical structures of science closely suit experimental data and experimental procedures.

> [...] My own attitude, starting with (Suppes 1962), is to go as deeply as possible into the actual practices of science at the level of measurement, observation, and computation, and how they should be reflected back into theory when the limitations imposed by errors or environmental variations are taken seriously. (Suppes 2011, 125)

The attention to the theoretical side of scientific theories and scientific change should be balanced with a critical examination of experiments and experimental procedures. This for Suppes is forcefully done with constant attention to the structure of theories, but the formal stance should be mitigated in treating the nuances of empirical practice in the analysis of the structure of scientific experimentation.

> In effect, you see, it is a disappointment to me that I haven't written a larger work on what I would call the foundations of data structures, the empirical side [...] Yet I think it's actually a failure on my part, but also a failure on the part of modern philosophy of science, not to have gone deeper into the analysis of the structure of scientific experimentation as practiced. (Frauchinger 2008, 171)

Hence, going back to the characterization of Suppes as philosopher of the details, we believe within this framework it is possible to reflect on the importance both of formalization and set-theoretical methods to represent theories and their limits, in particular in representing experimental procedures. The fact of being so attentive to details leads Suppes to introduce set theory and set-theoretical structures to give a more realistic view of scientific theories, without leaving out all the mathematical particulars that are necessary in a philosophy of science which dares to be rigorous and precise. However, the same attention to details brings Suppes to reject the idea that set-theoretical methods can be sufficient for a satisfying analysis of experimental procedures. This tension between the desire toward abstraction and the attention to data, between the construction of formal theories and the detailed analysis of empirical results is balanced by Suppes' pragmatic attitude which, from the one side, is a consequence of this same tension and, from the other side, is at the roots of it.

1.3 Pragmatism

The peculiar relation between formalization and attention to the empirical dimension is very close to a pragmatist approach to philosophy. However, the term 'pragmatism', when referred to Suppes, can be intended in two senses. The first one is a general pragmatic attitude, for which every scientific activity must be seen as a perpetual problem solving and scientific theories are local and created to solve a specific set of problems (Galavotti 1994). The second sense is a more specific philosophical trend like traditional pragmatism, namely the philosophical school of authors like Charles Sanders Peirce, William James, and John Dewey.

The first type of pragmatism is for Suppes the natural evolution of his attention to the way science is practically carried out. If we think of physics, and the way physicists perform their daily activities—Suppes points out—the focus is on practice as opposed to foundations. According to Suppes (1998), pragmatism reigns in physics in three different ways. First because physics is not committed to any form of foundationalism: not even theoretical physics operates in an axiomatic fashion. This is mainly for practical reasons that have to do with the way in which theoretical physics is carried out at the edge of what is technologically possible, where philosophical claims about certainty of observations are sort of fantasies.

The second way in which pragmatism enters in physics has to do with the mistaken hope to give a kind of foundational account of physics (in particular experimental physics) and to the fact that physicists should behave in accordance with that.

> [...] The hope of giving any kind of complete foundational account is quite mistaken. Mistaken in the way it would be to give a set of axioms for playing tennis that were meant to be in any way adequate to lead to descriptions of actual tennis games. (Suppes 1998, 237)

The third way for speaking of pragmatism in physics is the accordance existing among theoretical and experimental physicists about the truth or falsity of the observations made. This accordance derives from a common background on which there is basically no disagreement amongst physicists.

For Suppes the detailed analysis of examples taken from physics is a continuous proof that the attitude of physicists is highly pragmatic, as it is evident for example by observing the orientation toward probability of the physicists who worked on quantum mechanics in the early days.

> Their wholly pragmatic attitude toward probability is evident. They didn't really see it as necessary, in any sense whatsoever, to make a commitment to a foundational view, but they understood very well that the computational aspects of probability were exactly what they needed for the new theoretical treatment of quantum phenomena. (Suppes 2006, 36)

So, starting from the acknowledgment of this very concrete pragmatic attitude, Suppes' interest in pragmatism becomes stronger while moving away from the more foundationalist view of science at the beginning:

> In early years, I was put off by what seemed to be the relatively superficial philosophical doctrines of pragmatism. They seemed to be lacking in depth and, perhaps to make a joke, any serious model theory. With the modern move away from foundations as an explicit aim of most philosophical work in the sciences or mathematics, I have come to see that pragmatism fits very well. It is fair to say [...] my thinking about this relationship for a very long time was in terms of constructing explicit formal structures that gave a detailed sense of how a particular part of science would look when given the kind of explicit treatment characteristic of that given structures in modern mathematics. My 2002 book gave a good many examples of this. I am not against those examples now, but already as I was writing the final version, I found myself moving toward pragmatism. (Suppes 2006, 35)

This movement toward pragmatism has been supported not only by the observation of pragmatic attitudes in the empirical science, but also by a closer acquaintance with the classical philosophical pragmatism, and the beginning of a deep reflection on it, in particular on some authors like Giovanni Vailati (Arrighi et al. 2009).

The new conception of experience carried out by classical pragmatists is at its top in Vailati's view:

> Practice plays a constituent role in experience, which is always active and inferential, shaped by interaction with surroundings and the corre-

sponding habits or expectations. (Caamano and Suppes 2009, 23)

Moreover, Vailati rejects anything that can be considered as 'hard data', giving back a conception of experience which is active and constantly construed in accordance with pragmatic reasons. It is easy to recognize the very same conception also in Suppes who, starting form his famous 1962 paper (Suppes 1962), introduces the concept of 'models of data' and recognizes that different pieces of information count as 'data' depending on the level of abstraction required for the specific purpose at hand. More generally, it is easy also to see that the features listed as characteristic of a pragmatic epistemology—in particular anti-foundationalism and fallibilism—perfectly holds for Suppes' epistemology as well (Caamano and Suppes 2009).

In reflecting on Suppes' pragmatism, we must not miss Ernest Nagel's influence as Suppes' mentor. Nagel had a very deep intellectual debt to Dewey, derived from the interactions they had when they were both at Columbia University. Hence, it is fair to say that Suppes, by means of Nagel's influence, has a strong connection with traditional pragmatism. However, it is equally fair to say that Suppes moves away from it. Actually, in the traditional pragmatic literature there is not any discussion about precise and detailed scientific experiments; Peirce, for example, speaks only about theories and never about experiments, while Vailati is much more attentive to the experimental side, even if he does not present specific cases. In this sense, Suppes acknowledges some important insights coming from traditional pragmatism, but immediately moves further by declining them in a scientific perspective.

> So one of the theses is that the really nice instances of pragmatism are to be found in science. In philosophy people do not have the sort of special cases [. . .] the discussions are much more abstract and general level in philosophy of pragmatism, they aren't focused on critical examples, whereas the scientific discussions have the ability to focus on what are the pragmatic aspects, worked out in real theories and real experiments and what are pragmatic aspects of the history of a given scientific set. (Interview, 9 December 2006)

It is worth noting, moreover, that the pragmatic stance influences one of the very few reflections by Suppes on the debate on realism.

> Fundamentally, my attitude is pragmatic. Some objects I believe in, some I have questions about, and others I do not believe in. More im-

portantly, it is evident historically that objects come and go as processes do. This means there is a lot of stability in much, if not most, of the world. [...] So, what brand of realism have I just been describing as my own? Well, it is a kind of pragmatic realism that somehow cannot get excited about a good many of the controversies in the realism-antirealism disputes. (Suppes 2008a, 157)

Suppes' criticisms have shown the untenability of a conception of science as a big unitary and comprehensive framework, organized according to well established rules, that aims at giving a coherent and complete image of reality; thus room is left for a new vision of science, centered around a pragmatic attitude.

> It is my own view that a much better case can be made for the kind of instrumental conception of science set forth in general terms by Peirce, Dewey, and their successors. In this view, scientific activity is perpetual problem solving. No area of experience is totally and completely settled by providing a set of basic truths; but rather, we are continually confronted with new situations and new problems, and we bring to these problems and situations a pot-pourri of scientific methods, techniques, and concepts, which in many cases we have learned to use with great facility. (Suppes 1999, 484)

This pragmatic attitude is well exemplified by quantum physicists, who use the mathematical and computational tools of probability theory without any real philosophical commitment to probabilistic thinking, but just because such mathematical apparatus fits particularly well with their theories of quantum phenomena (Suppes 2002).

So, if it is senseless to expect from science a global picture of reality, we can also claim that scientific theories are not a collection of true sentences about some particular aspect of reality. But, again, if scientific theories are not meant to describe reality and are not concerned with truth, what are scientific theories for?

In Suppes' view they are a sort of pragmatic device that allows us to reason on the connection between sets of facts that appear to be somewhat related; they try to elicit the rules that allow us to predict the emergence of a certain kind of fact after having observed the occurrence of another kind of fact.

> The most important function of a theory, according to this view, is not to organize or assert statements that are true or false but to furnish material principles of inference that may be used in inferring one set of facts from another. (Suppes 1967, 64)

The recognition of this function of theories brings with it an important new criterion for the evaluation of scientific theories. It is no more possible to judge the value of a theory with respect to the accuracy in describing the reality, but rather what has to be evaluated is the usefulness of such a theory in connecting observed facts and in predicting new ones.

> [...] when theories are regarded as principles of inference rather than as major premises, we are no longer concerned directly to establish their truth or falsity but to evaluate their *usefulness* in inferring new statements of fact. (Suppes 1967, 64)

After having examined under Suppes' perspective what the function of a scientific theory is and how to evaluate the fitness of theories, we can conclude with a quotation from the famous 1967 paper titled "What is a scientific theory?". Suppes' answer is given in perfect behavioristic style and again is permeated with pragmatism:

> An adequate and complete answer can be given only in terms of an explicit and detailed consideration of both the producers and consumers of the theory. (Suppes 1967, 66)

So Suppes ends up with a very pragmatic attitude both on specific fields, such as his view on probability, and in general, as a view that prescribes the use of different kinds of methods for different purposes. A pragmatic agenda is for Suppes much more in accordance to scientific practice and, hence, to be further carried out in the representation of it. However, this pragmatic agenda must be revised in the light of a detailed approach to the study of science in order to specialize the too general analysis conducted by the classical pragmatists.

> In fact, I think philosophers really should push a more pragmatic agenda for science. It's surely much more faithful to scientific practice. But it must be sophisticated. William James, whom I much admire, advocated pragmatism as a philosophy, but his exposition was too simple, as a guide to science. Unfortunately, most of the philosophers who have written about pragmatism have not tangled with scientific matters in detail. A variety of pragmatic case studies of scientific practice would be a very desirable thing. (Frauchinger 2008, 174)

1.4 Pluralism

The just described pragmatic approach leads Suppes to refuse a comprehensive theory of science in favor of a pluralistic view of it:

> Like our own lives and endeavors, scientific theories are local and are designed to meet a given set of problems. As new problems arise new theories are needed, and in almost all cases the theories used for the old set of problems have not been tested to the fullest extent feasible nor been confirmed as broadly or as deeply as possible, but the time is ripe for something new, and we move on to something else. (Suppes 1999, 484)

Pluralism is not just neutrally observed in science, but it is considered by Suppes as a desirable feature to be applauded as the plurality of political views in a democracy.

Suppes claims that scientific knowledge has a local character and has to be analyzed within a specific context. A comprehensive theory of science cannot exist, especially if we look at its experimental side, and a pluralist attitude, in contrast, should be promoted.

> A lot of my examples revolve around policy issues and the resolution of action in policy questions; in general the resolutions are mostly inevitably pragmatic [...]. Experiments in science have the same feature: theories can be given an absolutely tight formulation in some sense, where experiments can't be; in experiments you can say something sharply, but lots and lots of procedures are not sharp, they're going to have practices, and anybody familiar with experiments knows how complicated much modern instrumentation is [...]. (Interview, 9 December 2006)

According to Galavotti (1994), as she pointed out in a paper presenting a characterization of Suppes' philosophy of science, the abandonment of the unity of science goes hand in hand with the rejection of the neopositivistic ideal or reductionism, intended in its most general sense as unification of the sciences as the one proposed in the *International Encyclopedia of Unified Science*. Pluralism concerns the language, the subject matter, and the method both in different disciplines and in different branches of the same discipline.

As it should be clear by now, Suppes moves from the insistence on the specificity of each single discipline towards the analysis of their logical and conceptual structure, but we cannot avoid once again to stress the fact that this does not lead to a uniformity of methods. In fact, he acknowledges that many disciplines resist an analysis solely conducted with the axiomatic method based on set theory, in that applying this pluralistic approach also to his own analysis; a paradigmatic case (given its abstract character) is that of theoretical physics:

[...] theoretical physics is concerned with problem solving, in strong contrast to theorem proving. The essential skill is knowing just what assumptions or empirical facts to draw upon. Formal axioms seldom, if ever, play a role. (Suppes 1997, 7)

Even in the use of the mathematical tools this discipline, like many others, is very peculiar. Talking about mathematics in theoretical physics Suppes says:

First, they are highly constructive, mainly calculational in character [...]. Second, they are fragmentary [...]. Third, the broad organization of the argument fits a problem-solving not theorem-proving style. (Suppes 1997, 7-8)

However, the refusal of a comprehensive theory of science must not be read as a weakness; in describing Suppes' philosophical view on science, we could speak of a *coherence* of approach. Of course this does not mean that there is just one method, like for example the set-theoretical axiomatization, to look at science, in terms both of its processes and its results. But it means that there is a coherent way to look at problems and notions "in a way that makes it possible to distinguish between their various components, and allows identification of structure at different levels of abstraction" (Galavotti 1994, 261). And this results in an approach in which both theories and data, mathematical results and experimental techniques play a central role. From these passages it is easy to understand that Suppes' pluralistic account is not exhausted by its defense of the plurality of the sciences, but also concerns the plurality of epistemological approaches that can be used in the analysis of the sciences, whose form strongly depends on the features of the discipline which is the object of analysis.

Another question which spontaneously arises is whether, given this pluralistic account, it is still possible to aim at having a complete theory of at least some large portion of reality. Again, unless we restrict our focus to very narrow portions of reality, Suppes' answer is negative:

It is apparent from various examples that weak forms of completeness may be expected for theories about restricted areas of experience. It seems wholly inappropriate, unlikely, and, in many ways, absurd to expect theories that cover large areas of experience, or, in the most grandiose case, *all* of experience, to have a strong degree of completeness. (Suppes 1999, 483)

But if science cannot reach a complete description and definition of reasonably extended parts of reality, we can infer that the purpose of science is no more that of knowing the ultimate reality, its activity rather consists in facing very specific problems that arise in the everyday practice of scientists, trying to offer solutions that are more and more satisfactory as long as science proceeds.

This reading of the progress of science is very far from the idea of a linear approximation to the full knowledge of the reality. We would rather say with Suppes that the progress emerges from the practices of science, in a constructivistic fashion. But there is of course another, stronger, sense in which Suppes' approach can be defined as constructivistic, a sense that is tight to its peculiar way of dealing with scientific theories, namely the semantic view approach. According to this, the enterprise of science consists in the construction of models that are more and more appropriate to represent the experimental evidence. More precisely, in the construction of hierarchies of models, ranging from formal models of the theory, to models of the experimental procedures, to models of data (showing how data are collected, filtered, organized and tested). In this sense philosophy of science not only *describes* how science deals with its own problems, but *constructs* a representation of scientific domains.

Again, it is the attention to details in the analysis of science that gives back a pluralistic view concretely translated in an anti-dogmatic, non-absolutist, and anti-foundationalist approach.

> I think that philosophers who look at science in detail can become acutely aware of vacuous generalizations in philosophy about the nature of thinking or about the nature of the world. The world turns out to be very complicated, very nuanced, and the philosophers who are going to tell us in a few words how it is, in a dogmatic way, will not in the long run be taken seriously. [...] Philosophers traditionally have sought to present a much bigger picture of the world than most scientist do, because a serious scientist understands how difficult that is, in terms of the many details he knows about his specialty. (Frauchinger 2008, 174)

With respect to this, Aristotle for Suppes illustrates exactly the opposite tendency. He is detailed, deeply involved in the scientific issues of his time, profoundly sophisticated, and with a lot of *nuanced* things to say. The role of the philosopher in providing a conceptual foundation and interpretation of the fundamental theories and experiments in science should prevent him from saying how things are and how the world works only in few words.

It is worth noting that Aristotle plays a central role for Suppes both in general, as the kind of philosopher able to give back a nuanced view of the world based on his wide knowledge of its details, and in particular, as inspiration for the new philosophical and scientific program Suppes has embraced in these latest years, that is a wholly new philosophy of mind and brain.

This revised agenda for philosophy of mind and brain is worth mentioning in this general introduction. It is, from the one side, the newest project which Suppes is working on, and, from the other side, it represents the *summa* of his ideas, approaches, and philosophical views.[1] The basic idea is that philosophy of mind should be more similar to, for instance, philosophy of physics and, hence, dominated by scientific findings in psychology and neurosciences about the nature of mind. The general interest in representation, and the specific interest in brain representations, has moved Suppes to what he himself defines as 'neuropsychological foundations of philosophy' (Suppes 2005, 144). Here Suppes believes that these philosophical matters should be treated as empirical and, hence, subjected to empirical investigations. This does not mean to exclude philosophy from the field, but rather to change its role for building the conceptual foundations of these scientific results.

> The building of such a foundation is itself as much scientific as philosophical. What marks it as philosophical is the emphasis on a certain range of concepts, some of which may remain controversial and will not be clarified for some decades by proper theoretical and empirical scientific findings. (Suppes 2008b, 19)

After all, this is completely in line with Aristotle's approach, that mixed science and philosophy of his time. But this accord does not concern only the method, but also the content, as it is evident by looking at Aristotle's *De Anima*, as Suppes does in his new agenda for the philosophy of mind. Aristotle emphasized that mind is not separate from the body, but that is the form of the body, namely it is embodied.

---

[1] Despite the importance of this field, we have chosen not to devote a whole chapter of the book to this topic, since it is still an ongoing work, full of scientific details difficult to understand and to explain in a limited space. However, given its importance, throughout the book we will sometimes refer to this research.

In other words, mind expresses the form and the functions of the body from a mental standpoint (Suppes 2008b). So Suppes is involved in a program that has its roots in the Aristotelian biological approach to mind, in contrast with the Cartesian one.

It is worth noting that, also within the latter new program, formal methods, empirical details, historical background are all central in Suppes' approach. As a matter of fact, this program is rooted in Aristotle, and Hume as well, so with a strong historical reference that frames the whole debate. Moreover, it is a program based on the analysis of a huge number of empirical data, so with a constant attention to empirical details. Finally, it aims at a formal representation of brain processes, so with a large employment of set-theoretical methods.

1.5   Antireductionism

All throughout this work we will many times emphasize how the core of Suppes' philosophy of science resides in his methodological approach to the study of the sciences, starting from the axiomatic method, to the use of probabilistic tools, to his active participation in the scientific enterprise.

The fact of supporting such a conviction in the centrality of methodological issues may communicate the wrong impression that Suppes postulates some sort of unity of science, based on a unique scientific method. On the contrary, this is something Suppes strongly rejects.

Most of the defenses of the idea of the unity of science are based on reductionism, namely on the possibility to reduce one science to another. Such reduction has been hypothesized in various ways. Suppes' criticisms in (Suppes 1999) concentrate on three forms, that are probably the most common ones: reduction of language, reduction of subject matter, and reduction of method.

The first form of reduction that Suppes takes into consideration is that of language: the advocates of this sort of reductionism claim that if scientists, especially those working on close or related disciplines, could try to translate the technical sentences explaining their theories in a common and possibly simpler language, this could enhance cross-fertilization between domains.

Obviously Suppes is not against such intellectual exchange, but he does not hold that this can be obtained through a neglect of the specificity and the technicalities of the different disciplines.

Part of my thesis about the plurality of science is that the languages of the different branches of science are diverging rather than converging as they become increasingly technical. (Suppes 1999, 478)

Not only this: more strongly, Suppes claims that the specificity of the languages of the different branches of science must be defended, as it is a source of enrichment in the end:

The irreducible pluralism of languages of science is as desirable a feature as is the irreducible plurality of political views in a democracy. (Suppes 1999, 478)

A stronger position of reductionism that Suppes also contrasts is the one related to the subject matter of the sciences. According to this position, when the study of elementary particles composing matter will have reached its full maturity, all the relevant researches will be those directed towards the ultimate physical entities composing matter, since every macroscopic object of inquiry will be in the end reducible to its infinitesimal components.

But it is exactly the study of these infinitesimal components of reality that is showing day after day the uselessness of this enterprise: on the one hand, as observational instruments become more and more powerful, what have been believed to be the ultimate components have every time revealed to be themselves composed by more elementary particles. On the other hand, the relations between matter and energy are not clear at all: we still cannot be sure whether objects are composed by swarms of particles or particles made up of swarms themselves.

In Suppes' view it is senseless to think about reducing all the sciences to the study of the ultimate components of reality given that it is not clear at all whether we could ever be able to pick up what those ultimate entities are:

To put the matter in a skeptical fashion, we cannot have a reduction of subject matter to the ultimate physical entities because we do not know what those entities are. (Suppes 1999, 479)

One could say that, even if not to the ultimate physical constituents of reality, we could reduce the subject matter of sciences at least to physical reality as a whole.

Even in this case, Suppes' reply is negative and he shows this with two examples (Suppes 1984). The first one is relative to the impossibility of reducing the software to the hardware of a computer, and the second (very similar) one is the impossibility of reducing mental phenomena to physiological ones.

The first example shows that the features of a computer program are completely independent from the hardware in which it is implemented:

> Whether my computer is made up of vacuum tubes, old-fashioned transistors, densely packed silicon chips, Josephson junctions, or optical devices makes no real difference as far as essential features of a program are concerned. (Suppes 1984, 130)

The second example is conducted in parallel with respect to the first and is relative to the irreducibility of mental states to physical states of the brain. Such irreducibility can, according to Suppes, be inferred by the fact that, despite the common physiological structure and functioning of the brain, different subjects display a very different mental life:

> Our brains have many common physiological characteristics, but the way in which the software of mental events is written in that hardware varies enormously from individual to individual. (Suppes 1984, 132)

An interesting thing, that it is worth reminding here is that the analysis of mental events has to be conducted with behavioristic means, first of all because mental activities of other individuals are not directly accessible, but also because many mental phenomena remain unaware (and some of these are very important for our survival, like those responsible for actions in which we are particularly skilled or for which we have formed an habit).

A last form of reductionism, that has probably received greater consensus than the previous two, is reductionism of method. The supporters of this position recognize that each branch of science has its own subject matter, theoretical formulation and instrumentation, but all branches share a common methodology, 'the' scientific method, something that holds throughout the different disciplines and that can be defined as a sort of step-by-step recipe that scientists working on different fields should follow.

But again the complexity of science stands against this pretense because the way in which theories belonging to different scientific domains are experimentally tested strongly depends on the theoretical assumptions and the instrumental apparatus, and are thus much varied and absolutely irreducible.

[...] it is especially the experimental methods of different branches of science that have radically different form. It is no exaggeration to say that the handbooks of experimental method for one discipline are generally unreadable by experts in another discipline [...] (Suppes 1999, 480)

A last criticism is directed by Suppes against a more general form of reductionism, according to which what all disciplines have in common and may then constitute a basis for reductionism is the dependence on sense data. Suppes sees some naivety in such a conception of sense data, as it completely disregards the complexity of the issue of what data really are, how they are collected and selected, possibly after having applied a theory of error and how much all of this is influenced by the theoretical framework the data should test.

The reduction of the analysis of experience to sense data is itself one of the grand and futile themes of reductionism, in this case largely driven by the quest for certainty. (Suppes 1999, 481)

Once that all forms of reductionism have been refuted, we can say that, as a consequence, the idea of the unity of science also collapses; having a unifying theory able to explain all the phenomena in the universe as a point of arrival for the scientific progress has been a dream of many scientists (Albert Einstein was among them), but it has shown to be quite unrealistic as a goal.

The recognition of the intrinsically plural nature of science legitimates the co-existence of different methods, languages, experimental procedures in the multifarious building of science.

There is no bounded fixed result toward which we are converging or that we can hope ever to achieve. Scientific knowledge, like the rest of our knowledge, will forever remain pluralistic and highly schematic in character. (Suppes 1999, 484)

1.6 Organization of the book

This book is organized in the following way: Chapter 2 presents the axiomatization of theories in terms of set-theoretical models as developed by Suppes starting from the 1950s, focussing on the concept of model and on its role for representation and invariance. Chapter 3 discusses Suppes' model view with respect both to the traditional linguistic view, as advanced by the logical positivists, and to the semantic view, emerged in the wake of Suppes' emphasis on models.

Chapter 4 focuses on the formal methods developed by Suppes, as well as on its historical roots and the meaning and limits of this formalization. Chapter 5 analyzes experimental procedures in the light of set-theoretical models providing the key elements of Suppes' theory of experimental design.

2

Axiomatization of Theories and Set-theoretical Models

Axiomatization is a recognized approach in the philosophy of science to improve the rigor and clarity of its results. This axiomatic attitude, with the foundation of the various branches of physics, has also been at the core of Suppes' work since the beginning of his career in the 1950s'. From there on, Suppes has expanded his program by adopting formal methods for investigating other branches of science than physics. This investigation constitutes a completely new approach to the philosophy of science which, in the case of Suppes' proposal, adopts formal methods to analyze the foundations of scientific disciplines. Formal methods are identified by Suppes with set-theoretical methods: but what does it mean specifically that scientific theories can be axiomatized as set-theoretical predicates? To answer this question it is necessary to understand what an axiomatic characterization of theories is and, then, why formal methods are identified with set-theoretical methods. The purpose of this chapter is to show the nature of this approach and its motivations for being adopted as the best means to *represent* scientific theories with particular attention to detect their *invariant* terms.

2.1 "To axiomatize a theory is to define a set-theoretical predicate"

The title above is probably, among Suppes' slogans, the most famous, but it is nonetheless obscure enough to call for a detailed analysis. First of all: axiomatization. In two of Suppes' early papers (McKinsey and Suppes 1953; Suppes 1954), axiomatization already constitutes the core of his programmatic proposal. A scientific theory can be expressed by means of formal axioms: the more developed the discipline is, the better axiomatization works. For Suppes, axiomatization constitutes a particularly suitable way to represent scientific theories, as it is able to detect their invariant terms.

Here is what Suppes declares:

> I think the best way to put it is that the axioms are part of the definition. So, we have some set-theoretical stuff at the beginning we don't ordinarily call axioms and then what we think of it is as the substantive part of the definition: condition one, condition two, condition three and condition four that any structure has to satisfy in order to satisfy that definition. Those conditions we naturally call axioms. So, it's sort of interesting the word 'axiom' itself is not a formal concept, axiomatizability is because we can say what that means, but to say what the axioms are is a matter of labelling and it isn't fixed exactly how we do that. So, for example, if I have a structure and I say it consists of a non-empty set and a binary relation on that set, ordinarily I don't put that statement as an axiom, that's characterizing the class of structures or what Tarski would call—and I think it's a nice language—'the possible realizations' of the theory you have in mind. Possible realizations don't necessarily satisfy the axioms, but they have the right set-theoretical properties and nothing more. So we keep that characterization separate from the axioms for the theory. (Interview, 20 November 2003)

Suppes uses the axioms of set theory, instead of the more traditional tools of classical logic. More precisely, in (Suppes 1954, 245), he argues for a constructivist attitude in the philosophy of science: to give a clear and rigorous account of any empirical science, it is necessary to construct suitable representations that are achieved by formalizing it in elementary set theory. In the same paper he also provides a general methodological procedure for axiomatization in four steps.

1. One must single out which are the theories (often coming from other branches of science) that are presupposed by the theory at hand, as most of the times empirical sciences are built on top of other disciplines or use some apparatus developed in other scientific fields. In empirical disciplines (e.g. physics, psychology, and economics) not only logic and set theory, but also the standard portions of mathematics, are usually assumed in order to develop the axiomatization.

2. One must list all the primitive notions that constitute the scope of the science under consideration, highlighting their set-theoretical properties. If, for instance, we choose to axiomatize particle mechanics, the primitive notions are the set of the particles, the interval of elapsed times, the position, and the mass.

3. Having in mind these primitive notions, one must then list all the axioms that have to be satisfied by the theory. In other words, these primitive notions are highlighted by being expressed by axioms. Axioms are the primitive statements of the theory, from which it is possible to derive the other statements that are considered true of the theory.

4. One must provide an empirical interpretation of the theory so axiomatized, namely the axiomatized primitive notions must be interpreted in an empirical domain.

Even if this methodological procedure seems straightforward, axiomatization requires full attention, in particular in the case of empirical sciences. Moreover, there is a widespread skepticism about the possibility of axiomatizing empirical sciences; in Suppes' view this skepticism relies on a wrong assumption, namely on the belief in the existence of a sharp distinction between pure and applied mathematics. According to the standard view, the one promoted by the logical neopositivism, only pure mathematics is endowed with rigorous and precise formulations of the problems enabling the application of very complex calculations that remain reliable even in this complexity. Mathematics applied to empirical domains, on the other hand, is seen as a mere auxiliary tool for calculation over data that, being obtained by trial and error processes, are much less precise. Thus applied mathematics is interpreted as a work that proceeds by way of approximation. On the contrary, Suppes sees a substantial continuity in the domain of theoretical sciences, thus every sufficiently developed scientific discipline is suitable of being axiomatized, even though he recognizes that not in every case an axiomatic treatment is the most appropriate one.

It is difficult to predict the general future of axiomatic methods in the empirical sciences. Economists use them extensively. In any case, axiomatic methods are now widely used in foundational investigations of particular sciences, as well as in the pursuit of certain general questions of methodology, especially those concerning probability, statistics and induction. [...] A conservative prediction is that they will continue to be applied in foundational work throughout this century, even when surrounded by a context of informal philosophical or scientific analysis. Such a mixture of the formal and informal is to be found in all the chapters that follow. This is both desirable and necessary, in the sense that many significant ideas in the philosophy of science are not expressed in a way that makes them suitable to formulate in terms of systematic axioms. [...] But granting this, and I consider it important to do so, there remains much useful work to be done in clarifying the nature of theories, by examining as thoroughly as possible questions of representation and invariance of the structures satisfying the explicit theoretical axioms of different theories. (Suppes 2002, 49)

Besides the methodological procedure for axiomatization, another important issue to be dealt with is the choice of assumptions. Going a step backward, one should consider the fact that every scientific theory stands on the top of a number of implicit assumptions and most of the times these assumptions are left in a sense "hidden" in the formulation of the theory. Take as an example Newtonian physics, which is based on the assumption that space and time are fixed and used as a frame of reference to measure motion. Before Einstein, these assumptions were never questioned and, being taken for granted, they remained hidden in the formulation of the theory.

One of the merits of the axiomatic approach is that of unveiling these assumptions. Once that light has been shed on them, the justification of the choice of some assumptions rather than others is put under focus. In the practice of science this choice is often left to intuition, but the application of the axiomatic method makes the assumptions explicit and thus calls for meaningful criteria of choice.

The first *desideratum* of axiomatization mentioned by Suppes is that assumptions are self-contained. Assumptions are the foundations of a theory, thus it is very important that all the assumptions are stated at the beginning of the development of the theory, since they will be the means to 'filter out' undesired consequences of the theory. It is also true that sometimes this task is very difficult and it can happen in science that *ad hoc* assumptions are added in a second moment. Nevertheless, this kind of addition should be avoided whenever possible: a high degree of rigor can be reached only if all relevant assumptions are clear and explicit from the beginning.

Another important insight in scientific theories is given by the possibility of singling out, in a theory, the minimal assumptions, namely, those assumptions that are sufficient to formulate that theory, but are not redundant. In order not to be redundant, these assumptions must be mutually independent, i.e. not deducible one from the other.

Being able to isolate the minimal set of assumptions is absolutely not trivial and it can give a measure of the deepness of the understanding of a theory. In another respect it is also a measure of the degree of development of the theory itself, as only in a theory thoroughly developed and understood it is feasible to separate what is fundamental and irreducible from what is spurious and inferable from something else.

2.1.1 Why axiomatization?

In (Suppes 1968), Suppes lists a series of very important consequences that strongly motivate the application of formal methods in general to scientific disciplines; most of these points hold also for the axiomatic method, as we will briefly discuss in this subsection.

Generally, the most important positive import from axiomatization is related to foundational issues: axiomatizing a theory amounts to giving an explicit foundation to that theory and this for sure contributes to the clarification of the concepts used in the theory. This work of clarification is at the core of a philosopher of science's tasks and that is precisely the reason of Suppes' insistence on the axiomatic method.

Going a bit deeper into details, what can be noted is the role of axioms with respect to the main concepts of a theory. What axioms do is to make explicit which are the properties of these concepts and the relations holding among them. Often discussions in philosophy of science suffer from some confusion about the concepts at the core of scientific disciplines; the fact of making more explicit the characterization of these concepts helps enhancing the level of the philosophical discussion.

It is important to notice that the greater level of communication is favored by the adoption of a single methodology for different scientific domains. This means that the mutual comprehension between scientists coming from different areas can be not only linguistic but, more importantly, operational. This is definitely not a minor issue, since, given the fact the Suppes rejects the usual idea of unity of science, to standardize language and methodology in this way is the only possibility to give a vision as uniform as possible to the multifarious and intrinsically plural enterprise of science.

The axiomatic method, when applied to science, gives another important insight: it gives a general picture of a scientific theory. Scientific theories are very complex entities: especially when they are in lively phases, they can be influenced by many extrinsic factors, derived from the specific way in which parts of the theory have been conceived. For instance, a theory can be expressible via different notations and the choice of one or the other can be due to sociological reasons. This means that this specific feature is inessential to the theory and it is pruned out by giving an axiomatic characterization of the theory itself. Thus, in a way, the axiomatization preserves the general and essential features of the theory by putting them in the front and leaving the inessential in the background. The metaphor Suppes uses is "seeing the forest in spite of the trees" and this renders also the idea of the power of axiomatization in expressing the general structure of a theory, that can otherwise be lost in a multitude of details emerging from the work of the practitioners.

Tightly connected with the issues of standardization and generality, is the one of objectivity. Here, again, one must not forget that the notion of objectivity Suppes refers to is a weak one: in his vision objectivity is not realized by a supposed correspondence between scientific theory and the real phenomena represented by the theory. Objectivity lies in the correspondence between different scientific theories describing the same phenomena: whenever it is possible to show an isomorphism[2] between two theories that are equivalent to a certain degree, this means that the two theories show a level of accordance; it is this accordance that expresses objectivity in Suppes' sense. Given this very restricted notion of objectivity, the axiomatic method is particularly important, as it is a very powerful tool in solving controversies about the interpretation given by different theories to very large amounts of data. Sometimes it is possible to show that controversies that are thought to be based on objective grounds are in fact only apparently objective, as the opponent theories can be proven to be isomorphic.

---

[2]For a more detailed explanation of the notion of isomorphism, see Section 2.3.1. Here it should suffice to say that the two theories are isomorphic when they have the same form, as expressed by their axioms.

These direct advantages descending from the axiomatization of scientific theories are already sufficient to motivate the choice of this methodology in the philosophy of science; nevertheless, it is worth mentioning also a series of indirect benefits, that are relevant and have been exemplified in (McKinsey and Suppes 1953).

If we go back to the issue of the choice of assumptions, we can recall that axiomatization makes explicit the hidden assumptions of a theory and favors the reasoning about the rationale for the choice of exactly those specific assumptions. Among the possible reasons for this choice, those connected to implicit conventions, i.e. those that do not intrinsically descend from theoretical motivations but are rather connected with pragmatic reasons (like conventional use), are particularly interesting. Very often in empirical theories assumptions are chosen that do not comply with the principles mentioned above, namely with self-containment and minimality requirements, but are formally or mathematically more convenient. Thus, in some cases the choice is made not on the basis of empirical, but rather of arithmetical considerations (for instance, a theory using a well known calculus can be preferred). This can be shown through axiomatization, that in this way uncovers implicit conventions. In other terms, once that isomorphism between two theories has been shown, from a pragmatical point of view the two theories can be considered as equivalent and thus the choice to embrace one or the other ends up in being somewhat arbitrary, conventional.

Another relevant issue in the philosophy of science is that of reducibility of theories. Usually, a theory is said to be reducible to another when the main laws of the former are consequences of the laws of the latter. Questions about reducibility are often not trivial, as it is not easy to compare different branches of scientific disciplines, but once that these branches are axiomatized the task is simplified, as the laws of both disciplines share a common framework. Take for example quantum chemistry and quantum mechanics: in order to understand whether one is reducible to the other (which, according to Suppes, is not the case), we need a common framework to be able to compare them: axiomatization offers this common ground. A further problem that is commonly encountered when the question of reducibility is applied to theories in empirical sciences is that often no sharp distinction is made between empirical facts and theoretical assumptions; such a distinction results once the theory is axiomatized and the assumptions are thus made explicit. Isomorphism (see Section 2.3.1) between theories is a direct and precise way to answer to reducibility questions.

Moreover, standard philosophical problems that are traditionally dealt with in the study of scientific theories can be seen under a new light when such theories are axiomatized; this is because the rigor required by formal methods forces also philosophers of science to pose their questions in a clearer and more effective way.

Finally, the effort required to axiomatize a theory gives as a result the emergence of new philosophical problems: this is because the imprecision can hide many problematic issues that become evident as soon as the theory receives a rigorous treatment. It is fair to say that in Suppes' view the axiomatic method has a strong heuristic value: the axioms give a new way to think about the subject and so they are a perfect means both for mature disciplines and for disciplines still at very early stages.

2.1.2   Why set theory?

It is fair to say that a theory has, as main objectives, to represent complex phenomena and, possibly, to reason about them. In order to describe as precisely as possible these phenomena, it should be able to express their main properties.

Axioms list the most important properties that the entity the theory is about must possess in order for it to satisfy the predicate to be defined. In other, simpler terms, when someone wants to give a definition of a certain 'notion', be it referred to a mathematical but also to an ordinary object, he or she gives a list of the properties this object must possess in order to be identified by that notion. For instance, if someone wants to know what a traffic light is, what one usually does is list some properties, like being of a certain shape, a certain color, being positioned in some special place etc., that an object must posses to be identifiable as a traffic light. The function of axioms in an axiomatic theory is exactly that of expressing in explicit terms the necessary properties that an entity must possess to be identified with the scientific concept at stake constituting its definition. These entities are what can be called 'primitive concepts' of a theory, whose properties are expressed in the axioms. As Suppes clearly states:

> The first point to recognize in axiomatizing a theory is that some concepts are assumed as primitive. Their properties are to be stated in the

axioms, and, therefore, it is important to know how many such concepts there are and what is their general formal character, as relations, functions, etc. (Suppes 2001a, 1027)

Being the selection of the relevant axioms of a theory the first step of Suppes' approach, the second one is their being expressed as set-theoretical predicates. We could say, in a way, that axiomatization is the methodology chosen by Suppes, while set theory is the preferred instrument to apply such methodology.

But why set theory and what is a set-theoretical predicate? The latter question is relatively easy to answer. A set-theoretical predicate is a predicate defined within set theory in a completely formal way (Suppes 2002, 32). In other words, the predicate is defined in terms of the notions of set theory. For example, to present classical mechanics, Suppes gives the following definition "A system of classical mechanics is a mathematical structure of the following sort ... " where the dots are replaced by a set-theoretical predicate (for further details see Suppes (1960) and Section 2.2). The set-theoretical predicate defines the entity under investigation, while the axioms express the properties of this entity. But, apart from being set-theoretical, which are the features of such a predicate? For example, is it necessarily a one-place predicate?

> Of course, from a formal standpoint you can certainly have a five-place, a six-place or a ten-place predicate, depending on how complicated the theory is, but I think it's very natural and generally considered more elegant to have a one-place predicate, because then you are making clear that what satisfies the theory is exactly the structure. There is one structure satisfying the theory. If I axiomatize groups in terms of... I say, 'a set A, a binary operation ∘ are together a formal group or group structure if and only if the following axioms are satisfied'... it's awkward. I have to talk about all these pieces of the structure. So it's much better to have a single entity to talk about; it's kind of metaphysically more elegant, I think. It's not too important! By the way, many mathematicians would want to ignore the distinction, they just want to talk about a set being a group being a set. Say, you have a set A, then you have an operation on this set; so this being very particular about the structure, the exact characterization of the structure is a kind of question that foundation folks like, you know? (Interview, 20 November 2003)

Less easy is to answer the former question, namely the reason of the emphasis on set theory. Surely, the set-theoretical framework is required in order to express the complexity of most scientific theories.

Standard formalization (namely the one using first-order logic) is not able to reflect the mathematical character of many scientific theories. It is not by chance—Suppes claims in (Suppes 2002)—that standard formalization has been widely used by philosophers of science, often at ease only with very simplified examples of scientific theories. But Suppes' aim is to represent, and reflect on, *real* complex scientific theories and there first-order logic manifests its limits.

We could think that maybe it is Suppes' closeness to the semantic view approach (see Chapter 3) that drives him towards the use of set theory. But is the semantic view approach compatible also with first-order logic? Asked directly, this is Suppes' reply:

> Well, I think so. There are special problems that are only going to be solved in first-order logic. A good example is the axiomatizability problem. Put another way, can you characterize certain classes of structures in first-order logic, that is, by elementary means? Some you can, some you cannot. And of course the interesting ones in many ways are the ones you show you have a proof that you cannot axiomatize. Because of course it is usually more difficult to give a proof that you cannot than to exhibit an example that you can. So, it takes more subtle analysis to get a non-axiomatizability result. For that purpose first-order logic is very useful. As far as you need distinctions about the semantic viewpoint for axiomatizability results, I don't see any, because I think that the structures that are models of a first-order theory are the same structures as those for a theory characterized by a set-theoretically defined predicate corresponding to the first-order theory. (Interview, 20 November 2003)

It is worth noting that the choice of this precise formalism is not 'forced': for Suppes it is just a matter of pragmatics, a good compromise between simplicity and expressiveness. In fact, the formalism must be simple in order to be 'workable' for philosophers who may be unfamiliar with mathematical technicalities, but at the same time the formalism must also be able to express the mathematical concepts which are useful for the scientific disciplines that are objects of philosophical study.

Starting from the 'simplicity requirement', Suppes shows that some very elementary theories are axiomatizable in first-order logic, as for example some theories of measurement, but as soon as things get more complicated, first-order fails, showing that this requirement is not sufficient for determining the choice of the right formalism. For instance, in (Suppes 1992), he shows that attempts to prove the finite axiomatizability of theories of measurement in a first-order framework fail (see Lindström's theorem[3]); though this is clearly a negative result, nonetheless it is significant for the philosophy of science, as it shows the limits of the logical instrument that is used and call for a different treatment. Within first-order logic it is not even possible to demonstrate that the theory at hand is in fact a theory of measurement with infinite models. This is because infinite models call for a condition which is not expressible in first-order logic, a condition which is necessary in order to show homeomorphism to numerical models, exactly what is required for a theory to be a theory of measurement. Thus Suppes concludes that:

> Almost all systematic scientific theories of any interest or power assume a great deal of mathematics as part of their substructure. There is no simple or elegant way to include this mathematical substructure in a standard formalization that assumes only the apparatus of elementary logic. (Suppes 1992, 207)

These reasons determine Suppes to prefer set theory, augmented by some axioms.[4] More precisely, such axioms are used to reason about the existence of the sets that are introduced in the universe. This is done in order to avoid paradoxes, which is especially important when dealing with scientific disciplines (Suppes 1972). For this reason, Suppes' approach is a refined kind of set-theoretical axiomatization, the refinements consisting in the consideration of the existence of sets. This is because the acceptance of the existence of every set whatsoever brings with it paradoxes and inconsistency problems (take for instance the set whose only member is the set itself, a typical paradox of set theory).

To better understand the role of set theory in axiomatization let us consider, for example, group theory. Informally a group is a nonempty set with a binary operation that satisfies certain axioms. These are the axioms of group theory expressing the properties that a mathematical object must possess in order to be defined "a group". The three axioms of the group theory are:

---

[3]In mathematical logic, Lindström's theorem states that first-order logic is the strongest logic (satisfying certain conditions, e.g. closure under classical negation) having both the (countable) compactness property and the (downward) Löwenheim-Skolem property.

[4]On the inconsistency of intuitive set theory, see (Suppes 1960).

A1 $x \circ (y \circ z) = (x \circ y) \circ z$
This axiom says that the operation $\circ$ (called the "group opera-tion") on the set A is associative;

A2 $x \circ e = x$
This axiom says that if one applies the operation $\circ$ on the element e and whichever element x of A the result is again x (and that's why e is called the "identity element");

A3 $x \circ x^{-1} = e$
This axiom says that if one applies both the $\circ$ and the $^{-1}$ oper-ations to whichever element x, the result is the identity element e (and that's why $^{-1}$ is called the "inverse operation", inverse with respect to the $\circ$ operation).

Given this, a group is an abstract structure which can have many concrete realizations: the set of natural numbers together with the ad-dition operation is perhaps the simplest example. The axioms are part of the definition of the predicate "is a group". They are the most im-portant part of the definition of this predicate. What do these axioms state? That an object, in order to be called a "group", must satisfy these axioms. What kind of object is this? It turns out that it is an algebra, namely an ordered quadruple composed by a set, A, an operation, $\circ$, another operation $^{-1}$, and an element e such that the axioms hold.

Once again, we recall that the choice of set theory is made for con-venience and pragmatic reasons. The crucial issue is axiomatization, while set theory is the specific framework within which to express this axiomatization. Furthermore, Suppes wouldn't subscribe an approach 'blindly' adherent to set theory as, in his opinion, not all entities can be reduced to sets. To maintain a certain flexibility *creative definitions* (of identity) are introduced.

The use of the adjective 'creative' is due to the fact that new propo-sitions can be proved in the theory once these definitions are added. Suppes puts it very precisely:

> I call this last definition *creative* because under rather weak assumptions we can show that something new can be proved using the definition. (Suppes in press, 4)

Creative definitions are used in order to introduce new abstract objects in a certain universe; these can eventually constitute a new category on their own and can then be potential members of sets.

Through the use of creative definitions one can, in a sense, create entities as needed and disregard—as irrelevant—the set-theoretical properties that would otherwise be implied if they were treated as sets. This allows us to concentrate on essential features of the defined object, which are not necessarily set-theoretical or mathematical in character.

Nonetheless, one should avoid the use of creative definitions as much as possible, in order to keep high standards of rigor.

> The ordinary requirement is that to be an honest definition, it should not be creative. It's a sort of criterion of merit to have a definition be non-creative. So, in that sense you reverse the ordinary sense of the value terms, but it's like being a creative accountant: you don't want your accountant to be creative, you want him to be accurate, you know, the same sort of thing. You don't want him to be creative with your bank account, for example. So [...] two criteria: a definition should be non-creative and it should be eliminable. So you could always eliminate it in favor of prior notions. That makes it really an honest definition. Now, of course there are a lot of places in mathematics where conditional definitions are used and their satisfying these two criteria is limited. So a conditional definition may be given so that only when the conditions on the conditional definition are satisfied can you prove it is non-creative.
>
> [...]
>
> You introduce a definition that is non-creative, for example, a typical thing is you define an operation that is not unique and then in the theory you can prove a contradiction. If definitions are non-creative and eliminable you can prove a general theorem that the theory is consistent, the addition of these notions will not make it inconsistent. So, that's the kind of purpose. Now, the creative definition or the non-creative one, introduces new notation; so, if you introduce that, from a formal standpoint the definition, creative or non-creative, should be regarded as a new axiom. So, in that sense you have added something. So, if we think that way, when we do a definition in set theory, that definition introduces new notation, like the notation for real numbers and therefore, what we want to be sure of is that the way we do that is non creative, so that we don't add anything to the stream for set theory. So we introduce the definition of real numbers in such a way that we can prove something that with the old notation we couldn't prove by going through the definitions but eliminating them at the end by the formulation of the theorem and that would be creative indeed. (Interview, 20 November 2003)

A similar point is reached in Suppes (in press):

> The point of introducing a new term is to facilitate deductive investiga-
> tion of the theory, but not to add new content to it. Two criteria which
> make more specific these intuitive ideas about the character of defini-
> tions are that (i) a defined term should always be eliminable from any
> formula of the theory, and (ii) a new definition does not permit the proof
> of relationships among the old terms which were previously unprov-
> able; that is, it does not function as a creative axiom. (Suppes in press,
> 2)

Finally, using set theory allows Suppes to give a uniform treatment
to very different domains, like that of pure mathematics and that of
physics.

> We think of it as being a predicate we introduce as a new formal def-
> inition within set theory. Like I start with set theory and set theory is
> of course nothing but a wonderful panorama of definitions, because
> we get everything from just a single, primitive notion of membership.
> So, this is another definition and that's why from a formal standpoint
> there's no separation between a physical theory and a mathematical the-
> ory under this viewpoint: both are characterized formally by a defini-
> tion of the structures that satisfy that theory, by such a definition be-
> ing given in set theory. So, to define systems of classical mechanics is
> the same as defining, let us say, finite groups. (Interview, 20 November
> 2003)

2.2 The structure of scientific theories: not only axioms

Axiomatization and the choice of set theory result in a completely different perspective on scientific theories with respect to the traditional
one. A theory is presented by defining a set-theoretical predicate. For
example, classical particle mechanics is defined by the set-theoretical
predicate 'is a model of particle mechanics', where the model of the
set-theoretical predicate is a structure that satisfies the predicate itself. In other words, the axioms, expressed as set-theoretical predicates, are interpreted by means of models: models are what satisfy
the set-theoretical predicate. A model of a set-theoretical predicate is
a structure, more precisely a set-theoretical structure, that satisfies the
predicate. The structure of a theory is thus represented in terms of the
models of the theory. Models are to be intended here as all the possible
realizations in which the theory is satisfied. "When a theory is axiomatized by defining a set-theoretical predicate, by a model for the theory

we mean simply an entity which satisfies the predicate" (Suppes 1957, 253).

The concept of model is of central importance in Suppes' approach to the philosophy of science and it is intended in a very precise way. Generally models are seen as two different types of representations. On the one side, models can represent selected parts of the world, and in this case they are regarded as *models of phenomena*. On the other side, models can be representations of theories, namely they interpret the axioms of the theory, and in this case they are regarded as *models of theory*. According to Suppes, however, this distinction of functions is not so fundamental and the central notion of model is that given by Alfred Tarski: "a possible realization in which all valid sentences of a theory T are satisfied is called a model of T" (Tarski 1953, 11). This logical definition is for Suppes the central notion of model, from which the others derive: "I claim that the concept of model in the sense of Tarski may be used without distortion and as a fundamental concept in all of the disciplines from which the above quotations are drawn [biological sciences, social sciences, mathematical statistics, applied mathematics]" (Suppes 1960, 289).

We recall that in logic a model is what makes all the sentences of a theory true. A model is a possible realization of a theory in which the theory is satisfied. To be more precise, a model is a structure interpreting what the theory represents. Consider a very simple example: Euclidean geometry that consists of axioms and theorems that can be derived from those axioms. In this case a model of Euclidean geometry is every structure in which all the statements of Euclidean geometry are true. A structure is an abstract and mathematical entity composed of:

- A non empty set of individuals called the *domain* or the *universe* of the structure (U).
- An indexed set of *operations* on the universe (O).
- A non-empty indexed set of *relations* on the universe (R).

A structure is, thus, a composite entity consisting of objects, and operations and relations on these objects with the following form $S = (U, O, R)$. In other terms, a model is a particular structure consisting of some domains of entities and some relations defined over them and satisfying certain conditions (Moulines 2006). To say that a model is formally defined as a set-theoretical entity means that it is defined as a tuple consisting of objects, relations, and functions. Models serve to interpret the axioms constituting the theory: models are what satisfies the set-theoretical predicates, namely the axioms expressed with the language of set theory.

2.2.1 Constancy of meaning, difference of use

One could now ask why the logical notion of model is considered as more fundamental than others. What is the place that physical models, the ones more common in the empirical sciences and usually intended as representations of phenomena, occupy in this picture?

> [...] you axiomatize the models introduced in the empirical sciences characterizing them by some set-theoretical predicate and so that models should satisfy the set-theoretical predicate; that brings it within the Tarski kind of framework. Now, I state the most extreme example: engineers love to talk about models and they do in a very good way often a very useful way and, it seems very scholastic, but we could certainly do it; we could take an engineering book where they introduce a model, like a model for signal processing or whatever, a model for circuits and we could go through and axiomatize it in this formal way and we wouldn't have made any big formal difference, but we would have organized it in this way. And the people will think about models, I mean after all model has a kind of double meaning in the sciences because it originates with the idea of building a physical model, an embodiment, so to speak, of the theory and we can raise a question: is this an embodiment? But as far as I'm concerned, we would have characterized such an embodiment so that it satisfied the axioms. I certainly think of measurement, I like to think of the procedures of measurement, physical procedures of measurement, empirical procedures of measurement as satisfying the axioms of some theory of measurement. (Interview, 20 November 2003)

The construction of a set-theoretical model is not meant in any case as a replacement of the physical model, they are two different kinds of entity, used for different purposes.

> If you have a physical model you've got a concrete physical object there and, you know, in some intuitive way, that physical object has an incredibly large finite number of properties, but only certain of those properties are properties of the theory we are thinking about. So, a typical example that is sort of amusing, if you think of particle mechanics, then, if we take particles as represented by small balls or something, the color of those balls, if they have a color, they are small but big enough to have

a color, we never talk about and we can't talk about in the theory and yet this might be a very salient property of any model. Or we build the model, for example, of the theory and we paint it grey, with grey paint on, will not be meant to be, probably, exemplifying a concept in the theory. So, the physical model is very much richer, of course, than the mathematical model, the purely abstract model, which we can also define in this purely abstract way. But I think that what's important in physics and not sufficiently discussed is that you need to come down at the experimental level to actual physical models and so a physical experiment takes place, not a thought experiment, not a *gedanken* experiment, but a real experiment. In that real experiment, to track out that real experiment is a model of the theory is a real piece of work, I mean it's a very long and complicated discussion. I know for example, when I and de Barros published this article on quantum entanglement where we derived new inequalities of what is called the GHZ situation about three particles (that's Greenberger, Horne and Zeilinger) what I think the editors liked who agreed to publish it in the *Physical Review Letters* was we spent a lot of time analyzing problems with the measurement equipment and probabilistic analysis of features of measurement procedures and it's that very detailed kind of analysis that is needed to take you from experiments all the way through to the question 'Do the data confirm the theory?' and not nearly enough is done of that kind. Most philosophers are, as we say, still in the parlor, not in the lab. (Interview, 20 November 2003)

To define formally a model as a set-theoretical entity which is a certain kind of ordered tuple consisting of a set of objects and relations and operations on these objects is not to rule out the physical model of the kind which is appealing to physicists, for the physical model may be simply taken to define the set of objects in the set-theoretical model. (Suppes 1960, 290–291)

Even though physicists are used to thinking that a model of, say, the orbital theory of the atom is something different from an abstract set-theoretical entity, however it is also true that the concept of a model in physics derives from logic the idea of being an interpretation or a realization of the laws constituting the physical theory.

The difference to be found in these disciplines is to be found in their use of the concept. In drawing this comparison between constancy of meaning and difference of use, the sometimes difficult semantic question of how one is to explain the meaning of a concept without referring to its use does not actually arise. When I speak of the meaning of the concept of a model I shall always be speaking in well-defined technical contexts and what I shall be claiming is that, given this technical meaning of the concept of model, mathematicians ask a certain kind of question about models and empirical scientists tend to ask another kind of question. (Suppes 1960, 289–290)

One way to think the relation between the set-theoretical model and a physical model is that of including the set of objects constituting the physical model in the set-theoretical model and then to interpret the relations in the set-theoretical model as real relations, such that a physical model is a special case of the set-theoretical model.

Consider Suppes' classical example (Suppes 1960): the axiomatization of classical particle mechanics in set-theoretical terms. This theory is axiomatized in terms of five primitive notions, thus resulting in an ordered quintuple $P = (P, T, s, m, f)$. P is a set of particles, T is an interval of real numbers corresponding to elapsed time, s is a position function defined on the Cartesian product of P and T, m a mass function defined on P, f a force function defined on the Cartesian product of P, T, and the set of positive integers. The ordered quintuple P is thus a model of classical particle mechanics. Clearly enough this theory is represented by the definition of a set-theoretical predicate—in this case the set-theoretical predicate 'is a model of particle mechanics'.

How this set-theoretical sense of model can refer to an actual physical model, in the sense intended by physicists? Take as an instance the 'solar system physical model of the atom'. Suppes answers this question in the following way:

The abstract set-theoretical model of a theory will have among its parts a basic set which will consist of the objects ordinarily thought to constitute the physical model. (Suppes 1960, 291)

Thus, the set of particles of the set-theoretical model can be considered analogous to the set of planetary bodies in the case of the solar system. Another possibility is to consider the set of particles as the set of centers of mass of the planetary bodies. The set-theoretical model is a sort of abstract structure that can be interpreted, from a physical point of view, in many different ways.

Another interesting remark Suppes makes is that more than one meaning can be ascribed to the locution "physical model": the latter can be intended as a physical simulation of the phenomenon under analysis, as well as the representation of the equipment used during the experiment, or a model of the measuring process used to collect data.

> If we mean by physical model a genuine physical model, that is really something in the real world, as a concrete object, of course these can be objects studied for experiments, you know, but other kinds of physical models are used in the experiments, like the measuring equipment would be another physical model, the theory is often not well understood by the physicists doing the experiment, because they haven't read the manual well enough and haven't called the technicians to ask them! So, I mean, physical model is either of two separate ways: as a physical model of the theory, then of course you think of the objects that are actually the focus of the experiment and that's how I think of the physical objects I mean, collections of atoms or what not, or one particular atom, you know, and how we get here is maybe a very tangled and subtle story. It won't be very straightforward in many cases. So, if you come in the room, you say 'where are the physical models?' You can't find them. (Interview, 20 November 2003)

But what is the nature of the objects that inhabit the abstract model? To answer this question, Suppes explains how one can characterize natural numbers by using set theory:

> For example, when you characterize the numbers, say the natural numbers, in terms of ϵ, then you are characterizing them in terms of some certain sets, which may have as sets only the empty set, or the set consisting of the empty set, or the set consisting of the set consisting of the empty set etc. [...] well, we don't need all that stuff and a different way to characterize is this: [...] you introduce simply the concept of the cardinality of the set. So, what is the criterion of identity for two cardinal numbers? Two cardinal numbers are identical, as abstract objects, if and only if two sets that have this property are equivalent in the ordinary isomorphic sense, with a one-to-one mapping from one set on to the other. [...] You can't even decide whether the number one is a set or not. That's undecidable. Now, I think myself we should use, as in this case, creative definitions of identity as a way to introduce objects. So, these are axioms, in other words, but they are creative definitions introducing new abstract objects. So, my other favorite example is ordered pairs. Well, it's classical in the history of set theory that two different definitions of the word 'pair' are given: one by Kuratowski, as I remember, and the other by Wiener. Now, both those definitions are for me unsatisfactory. The only feature about two ordered pairs, say (A, B)

and (C, D), so I have ordered pairs A first B second, then C first and D second in the other pair.... Those two ordered pairs are identical if and only if A is identical to B and C is identical to D. Nothing else is required. No funny sets need be introduced to characterize them. The sets have a peculiar asymmetric property that isn't needed at all. We just need a creative definition of identity. And so with abstract objects, we have clear answers of what are abstract objects. They have only the property that is given in the creative definition. There's nothing else to be said about them. (Interview, 20 November 2003)

We could say that the centrality of the set-theoretical notion of model lies in its ability to point out and to express the structure of a theory, besides all its practical details. The set-theoretical formalization expresses the meaning of the model of the theory in a technical and precise sense. When considering a set-theoretical model what really matters are the properties that are postulated in the model, and not the kinds of objects they apply to. They could be physical objects, they could be numbers, they could be ordered pairs of numbers.

What I have tried to claim is that in the exact statement of the theory or in the exact analysis of data the notion of model in the sense of logicians provides the appropriate intellectual tool for making the analysis both precise and clear. (Suppes 1960, 295)

The emphasis on models serves also for further purposes. The first one is relative to the independence of axioms. One of the major desiderata for a theory is that its axioms are independent, i.e. none of them is derivable from the others. Models allow us to verify whether this is the case. The test is straightforward: first, one finds a possible realization of the theory in which all the axioms but one are satisfied; if the one which is not satisfied is deducible from the others, then it would hold in the model, but in that case it would be both satisfied and not satisfied in the model, that is a contradiction.

But axioms are not the only thing whose independence can be proven thanks to the use of models. And here we come to another issue: models can be used to establish whether the primitive concepts of a theory are independent or not. In order to prove whether a primitive concept of a theory is independent from the other primitive concepts,

[...] it is sufficient to find two models of the theory, such that the domain of both models is the same, the two models are the same for all the other primitive concepts of the theory, but the two models differ only in their realization of the concept in question. (Suppes 2001a, 1028)

If these two models are found, the primitive concept is independent from the others.

A classical example given by Suppes to show the usefulness of axiomatization in terms of models when talking about scientific theory concerns the nature of measurement. Suppes, together with David Krantz, Duncan Luce, and Amos Tversky, have produced a three-volume treatise entitled *Foundations of Measurement*, whose first volume was published in 1971 (Krantz et al. 1971), the second in 1989 (Suppes et al. 1989), and the last one in 1990 (Luce et al. 1990). Suppes has devoted a great deal of his intellectual life to the foundational aspects of theories of measurement, starting from the beginning of the 1950's with his first published paper (Suppes 1951). A framework for the axiomatization of theories of measurement was given a few years later (Scott ånd Suppes 1958). Also in his intellectual autobiography (Suppes 1979a) he acknowledges a strong fascination for measurement from a methodological point of view. This area requires rigor and correctness of results in a field of analysis related to experimental and empirical procedures.

Without discussing any technical detail, the aim here is to show how an axiomatized theory of measurement allows us to pass from qualitative observations to the quantitative statements required in empirical sciences. Consider, for instance, to make the following observation (Suppes 1957): 'This rod is longer than that one'. How is it possible to infer the following quantitative assertion 'The length of this rod is 7.2 centimeters?' It is not possible to simply take a number and apply it to a physical object. This is an example of the general problem of the interpretation of quantitative notions needed in any advanced branch of science.

This passage from qualitative to quantitative requires an appropriate axiomatization. More precisely, the goal is to prove a representation theorem for the models of the theory (of measurement) establishing that any empirical model of the theory is *isomorphic* to some numerical model. We do not need now to formally define the notion of isomorphism and of two theories being isomorphic; here it is sufficient to stress that the concept of isomorphism makes the idea of same structure precise, i.e., the empirical models of a theory of measurement have the same structure as a numerical model. It is the existence of this isomorphism between models that justifies the application of numbers to things.

> The great significance of finding such an isomorphism of structures is that we may then use all our familiar knowledge of computational methods, as applied to the arithmetical structure to infer facts about the isomorphic empirical structure. (Suppes 1957, 266)

The advantage of the model-theoretic characterization of this concept (an empirical model being isomorphic to a numerical model) is to avoid all the difficulties connected to the expression of the same concept with a linguistic formulation. It is in this sense that the notion of model enters very naturally when discussing scientific theories in a detailed and precise way.

2.2.2   From scientific laws to hierarchies of models

Now it is fairly clear that, in order to have a theory of measurement, one needs to find a correspondence between an empirical model and a numerical model, but the connection between the model of a theory and the data that are recorded in an experiment has still to be explained.

According to what Suppes calls the 'received view',[5] the relationship between theory and data is quite straightforward: the axioms of a theory express scientific laws and theoretical terms are defined by means of observational terms. If we follow this approach, we can say that scientific theories are formed by two parts: a logical calculus and some rules to assign empirical content to the calculus; these rules are called *empirical interpretations* or *co-ordinating definitions*. These definitions can intuitively be seen as a linguistic expression of the correlation between theory and data; they express, with a linguistic correlation, the way in which the empirical data interpret the theory. In other terms, definitions are sentences which explain, often in a non formalized way, how data are to be read in order to be understood as an exemplification of what is said in the theory.

Let's try to explain the point with an example: take for instance an imaginary version of one of the experiments that are very popular nowadays in the neurosciences. Take two groups of individuals, the

---

[5]Suppes mainly refers here to Carnap's and Hempel's views; in other contexts, this is also called 'syntactic' or 'standard' view.

first composed by expert tango dancers and the second by beginners and measure their brainwaves while observing two people dancing tango in order to analyze whether there are similarities in the results of the measurements inside the groups and differences across groups. The experiment is conducted in order to show that the brain performs different activities (or activates different areas) according to the level of expertise of the subject in the activity he or she is observing.

Coordinating definitions, according to the received view, would be sentences describing how the results of the measurement of brainwaves relate to the theory about the activation of different areas of the brain.

In many of his works, for instance in (Suppes 1967), Suppes elaborates his own proposal moving from a contraposition with the just presented approach, which he also calls the 'traditional sketch' of theories.

In Suppes' opinion, these coordinating definitions are appropriate just for simplistic philosophical exposition of scientific theories, but are mostly unsatisfactory in the actual practice of science. This is because, in order to be able to relate theories and data, scientists need more sophisticated tools, namely formal models. As we have seen, models are not linguistic, but mathematical entities. So, primarily, scientists build models and only after having built these models they are able to write coordinating definitions; moreover, these usually do not deal with the relation between theory and experience, as philosophers of the traditional sketch use to claim, but only with the models of the experiment:

> Once the experience is passed through the [conceptual] grinder, often in the form of the quite fragmentary records of the complete experiment, the experimental data emerge in canonical form and constitute a model of the experiment. It is this model of the experiment rather than a model of the theory for which direct coordinating definitions are provided. (Suppes 1967, 62)

An attempt to explain the entire process could be the following: first the experiment is performed and some data are collected; these are usually somewhat confused and fragmentary. At this point they are 'conceptually filtered' and a model of the experiment is built out of them. It is this model that can be the object of coordinating definitions, which in a sense are about the coherence that data acquire once that they are filtered. The connection between this level and that of the theory is left out by the definitions.

Going back to the brainwaves example, first brainwaves are measured; if the sample is very big, the results will probably undergo a probabilistic treatment aimed at pruning out noise. Then they are 'filtered' through the 'expertise grinder' and the model of the experiment comes out; coordinating definitions are the linguistic description of this model rather than of the connection of the model with what was claimed in the theory; the connection between theory and data is much more evident if we compare the model of the theory of activation areas of the brain and the model of the experiment.

> The maddeningly diverse and complex experience which constitutes an experiment is not the entity which is directly compared with a model of a theory. Drastic assumptions of all sorts are made in reducing the experimental evidence, as I shall term it, to a simple entity ready for comparison with a model of the theory. (Suppes 1960, 297)

Anyway, in Suppes' approach the emphasis is on the shift from laws to models, the latter being the appropriate instrument to manage both theory and experiment, being both representable at different levels of abstraction, from empirical (more anchored to experience, more concrete) to numerical (more abstract) ones.

Moreover, in Suppes' view there is no more such a significant difference between theoretical and observational terms; the difference is given by the context rather than being intrinsic (Galavotti 2006, 214–215). In the example given before, both the theoretical and the experimental discourses are given in terms of brainwaves, but in the former case they are interpreted as a conceptual device, while in the latter they are a numerical result of a measurement. The conceptual device is the model of the theory, while the result of measurement is a model of data.

There is no more a sharp dichotomy between discourse about the theory and discourse about the experiment, rather there is a continuous process of successive abstractions that results in the emergence of a hierarchy of models: "exact analysis of the relation between empirical theories and relevant data calls for a hierarchy of models of different logical type" (Suppes 1962, 260). The 'basis' of the hierarchy is a very detailed model of the setting of the experiment and then, with a step-by-step process that abstracts from one parameter then from another, terminates with a model of the theory, in which only the basic concepts and their relations are represented.

In what follows we will elaborate more on the process that, starting from the data collected in an experiment, goes to the model of the theory, without loosing sight of the fact that the setting of the experiment and the way data are collected are not independent from the theory they are built to test.

2.2.3 From models of the theory to models of data (and back)

In a sense, we could say that for Suppes what is theoretical and what is observational is not given *a priori*, but sometimes it is also dependent on context.[6] As a consequence, there are no different methodologies that must be applied to the one or the other, but both must be dealt with in a similar way and, as we already know, this way is for Suppes represented by formal methods. "In moving from the level of the theory to the level of the experiment we do not need to abandon formal methods of analysis. From a conceptual standpoint the distinction between pure and applied mathematics is spurious"(Suppes 1962, 260).

Theories and data are strongly intertwined, there is thus a continuous interplay between these two components of science. Once again, the claim is that there is no sharp separation between the theory which defines a concept and the measurements that produce data relative to that concept; how much the theory influences the measurements is given by the empirical context (Suppes 1988a, 23).

In the same line of reasoning, one can say that even what data are can vary with context. In other words, data are not something which are neutrally given by experiments. The context provides the level of abstraction of what is scientifically relevant and thus determines what *counts as* data in a certain scientific theory.

> The "data" represent an abstraction from the complex practical activity of producing them. Steps of abstraction can be identified, but at no one point is there a clear and distinct reason to exclaim, "Here are the data!". (Suppes 1988a, 30)

In other terms, data are continually manipulated in successive operations of abstraction; a model of data is a particular interpretation (one, among many possible, that is shaped according to the theory

---

[6]The title of this section voluntarily recalls the title of (Suppes 2003a): *From Theory to Experiment and Back Again.*

that is going to be corroborated by data) that has undergone various processes of selection and analysis, starting from the very beginning, when the sample to be directly taken into consideration in an experiment is chosen (Suppes 1960).

Once that this sample is chosen, the experiment begins and some (also chosen) parameters are measured and from these measurements an observational model is built. These choices depend on a multiplicity of factors very difficult to isolate and to analyze in a systematic way; roughly speaking, they are connected to the background and intuitions of the scientist, even though the reference theoretical framework obviously plays a central role also in this choice. At this point, from observational models statistical regularities can emerge and from the pattern of these regularities, one can build empirical structures; then, starting from the empirical structure, one can build a theoretical model that fits the data. All these models, starting from the model of data, to the experimental model and so on, until the theoretical model, are arranged in a hierarchy.

But what are empirical structures? First of all, they are abstractions, in the sense that empirical situations are usually very complex and thus one has to choose which are the relevant details and abstract away from the rest, in order to build a structure. Once again, intuition and background assumptions have a key role in judging relevance.

In Suppes (1988a), a typology of empirical structures based on some elementary methodological distinctions is proposed. Such typology is used to show the different form and different levels of abstraction that empirical structures can assume. These levels can depend on the experimental techniques adopted in order to obtain the data, but even in cases in which these structures refer to the same experimental setting, they can represent it at very different levels of abstraction; Suppes himself illustrates this point with an example taken from measurement:

> As should be evident from this analysis, various empirical structures can be and are abstracted from the measurement procedures being carried out. One structure can include all the measurements $n_1, n_2, \ldots, n_p$. A second, more abstract one includes only the mean and standard deviation of the p observations. Still a third may include only the mean. In contrast, the laboratory record of the measurements can form the basis of a much more detailed empirical structure which includes the date and time of each measurement, the name of the experimenter, the la-

bel number of the balance and of the set of standard weights. (Suppes 1988a, 28)

A first methodological distinction is that between structures obtained by fundamental measurements and those obtained by derived measurements. Fundamental measurements are judgments about some property of a phenomenon to which a numerical representation is given, like in the case of an equal-arm balance. By contrast, the results of derived measurements are obtained by combining the results of other measurements. An example is that of the measurement of the momentum of a body, which is obtained by multiplying (the results of the measurements of) mass and velocity.

A further distinction is that between structures based on finite samples of data, like measurement of temperature at certain locations and in certain hours, and those based on continuous samples, like the continuous monitoring of seismographic activities to prevent earthquakes; obviously, the latter tend to be more complex and elaborate.

Finally, another remarkable distinction is that between structures built on data that are collected in order to test a theory and structures in which data are collected to test an hypothesis. Even in this case, the motivation underlying data collection influences the way in which data are collected and also which data are collected; this, in its turn, influences the resulting empirical structure.

The possibility of individuating a typology of empirical structures based on methodological concerns shows once again that the process of abstraction from data to theory is a very gradual one.

Another important point Suppes makes about the relation between theory and data is the importance of a so-called 'theory of error' (see the subsection 5.1.3 for a detailed exposition); his claim is that the way in which anomalies in observations are treated tells a lot about the maturity of a discipline. In fact, what is to be called an error is a matter of choice. How is this choice formulated? How many kinds of errors are there?

With respect to the first question, Suppes' answer is that the use of statistical methods is nowadays widespread both in experimental and in non-experimental studies and it is exactly statistics that can tell when an unusual datum has to be considered a mere deviation from the means and when it can be named an error.

Moreover, not all errors are the same (Suppes 2007a): when talking about errors, one immediately thinks at errors in making observations, but these are only a very specific kind of error; sometimes the parameters of the theory are intrinsically variable (for instance, they depend on time), sometimes the error reduces to the fact that the model of a theory does not fit with the data. Different kinds of errors have to be dealt with differently.

The recognition of the existence of errors of measurement in science and the attempt of studying the nature of these errors in order to have control over them and still maintain the solidity of science is one of the greatest contribution to sciences of the last two centuries. Such a contribution has become feasible thanks to the inclusion of probabilistic approaches in the scientific theories and practices (see subsection 5.1.3).

> It is fair to say that the explicit realization that errors of observation arise and yet that an explicit theory of these errors can be given is one of the main contributions of the theory of probability to general scientific methodology. Without such an explicit theory of error, much of the more exact and sophisticated science of the latter part of the 19th century and of the 20th century would have been conceptually difficult, if not impossible, in terms of serious confrontation between theory and data. (Suppes 1980b, 184)

2.3 Representation and invariance

So far, we have described the axiomatic method that Suppes applies to the philosophy of science, his approach based on set-theoretical models, and how this method can also be applied to empirical domains. In this closing section we will go to a more general level in order to understand what emerges of scientific disciplines after Suppes' approach has been applied to them. As we will see, what emerges are representations and invariants.

Set-theoretical axiomatization is, according to Suppes, the best way to represent scientific theories. But what kind of representation is that carried out by Suppes? It is a representation in terms of the *structure* of a theory, namely a representation devoted to detect its *invariant* terms. This structure is represented by means of the models of the theory, i.e. all the possible realizations in which the theory is satisfied.

Representation is clearly one of the central features of Suppes' approach. In 2002 Suppes published a book collecting many of his major results previously distributed over a large number of technical papers; this book (Suppes 2002) is significantly entitled *Representation and Invariance of Scientific Structures*, thus highlighting the unifying role played by representation and invariance in his work.

That of 'representation' is a central notion for science, as any scientific theory implicitly involves a series of choices on how to represent the phenomena that are studied in the branch of research the theory belongs to (Suppes 1988b). Representation, however, is a general concept and to better understand what has to be intended here by it, simple examples might be useful. Images, drawings or reproductions in different ways represent something, say an object. They can be used to show something about that very object because they, in a sense, 'stand on its behalf'. Images, drawings and reproductions give only partial representations of the object itself, in the sense that they focus on some aspects of the object and disregard some others. But it is exactly by focusing on some particulars that otherwise would be lost in the observation of the whole object in its complexity that it is possible to deepen the understanding of the object itself. In other terms, to represent something is to describe in a detailed manner some aspects of that something, thus providing an enrichment of the understanding of the object itself.

Representation can be seen also like a reduction of what is unknown (and thus object of analysis) to something that is known (or at least known better). In other terms, representations display a behavior that is known in advance by the person who built them. Once the relation between these means and what they represent is clear, this can simplify reasoning processes, as they can be conducted on things whose behavior is better known in order to obtain results that can be then applied also to something that is less manageable (the thing which is represented). This is because reasoning and experimenting on something which reproduces only the salient features of the object under analysis is easier and less expensive in many respects.

To give a very commonsensical example, if I want to reason on some feature of my car, say that I want to paint flames on its sides, I would probably make a drawing in order to understand how to fit the flames with the shape of the side of the car. In this case I would only draw a lateral view of the car and not one from the top or from behind. This is both because I do not want to 'be distracted' by something that is useless to my purposes and because drawing flames on a sheet of paper is easier and less time consuming than making proofs directly on the side of the car.

2.3.1 A formal approach to representation

In line with his general approach, Suppes develops a formal theory of representation, the core of which is the set-theoretical notion of *isomorphism of models*. Literally speaking, 'being isomorphic' means 'having the same form', so that, if we have two bricks which are made of a different matter, but have the same shape (form), we could say that they are 'isomorphic with respect to their shape'. Applying the concept of isomorphism to models, Suppes claims that "two models of a theory are isomorphic when they exhibit the same structure from the standpoint of the basic concepts of the theory" (Suppes 1988b, 256). From a technical point of view, to introduce the set-theoretical notion of isomorphism has the advantage to make the notion of 'same structure' precise (Suppes 1957).

Even though this definition is quite easy to understand, in (Suppes 2001a) he admits that it is a very hard—if not impossible—task to provide a definition of isomorphism which is valid for any kind of theory, so the usual practice is that of giving a different definition for every different scientific theory. For instance, in the case of a theory of measurement, what has to be sought is an isomorphism between some empirical structure and a certain mathematical structure.

From a more formal standpoint we present Suppes' example of definition for two algebras being isomorphic (Suppes 1988b; 2002, Ch.3). First of all an algebra is a structure $(A, \circ, e, ^{-1})$ if A is a nonempty set, $\circ$ is a binary operation from A to A, e is an element of A, and $^{-1}$ is a unary operation from A to A. An algebra $U = (A, \circ, e, ^{-1})$ is *isomorphic* to an algebra $U' = (A', \circ', e', ^{-1'})$ if and only if there is a function f such that:

- the domain of f is A and the range of f is A'
- f is a one-one function
- if a and b are in A, then $f(a \circ b) = f(a) \circ' f(b)$
- if a is in A, then $f(a^{-1}) = f(a)^{-1'}$
- $f(e) = e'$

We could say that isomorphism is 'axiom-free'. This means that the isomorphism of two models does not depend on the detailed nature of the theory, but only on the set-theoretical character of the models (Suppes 1967, 1988b). It could be possible for example to have two theories with their substantive axioms quite different, but whose models have the same set-theoretical structure, thus sharing the same definition of isomorphism.

A general argument in favor of the kind of axiomatization based on isomorphism emerges in discussing reductionism, and in particular in the case in which one branch of an empirical science can be reducible to another. Without attempting a general discussion of the meaning of reduction, Suppes claims that this notion might be formulated in a rigorous way by starting from the concept of isomorphism (Suppes 1954). If for instance one wants to defend the thesis that psychology can be properly reduced to physiology, he or she needs to show that for any model of a psychological theory an isomorphic model within some physiological theory can be construed (Suppes 1967). Clearly enough, the reductionist issues that cannot be stated in these clear set-theoretical terms are to be removed from the analysis.[7]

To analyze another example, again the theory of measurement can help to show how reasoning in terms of set-theoretical models, in particular in terms of isomorphism of models, can be useful. In order to pass from qualitative observations to quantitative statements, in the theory of measurement, it has to be demonstrated that any empirical model is *isomorphic* to some numerical model of the theory. This means that a representation theorem for the models of the theory should be proved.

What representation theorems do is to demonstrate that a certain class of models (that are chosen in virtue of their possessing some relevant features that are relevant for the theory) exemplifies, by means of an isomorphic relation, every model of the theory.

Perhaps the best and strongest characterization of the models of a theory is expressed in terms of a significant representation theorem. By a *representation theorem* for a theory the following is meant. A certain class of models of a theory distinguished for some intuitively clear conceptual reason is shown to exemplify within isomorphism every model of the theory. More precisely, let **M** be the set of all models of a theory, and let **B** be some distinguished subset of **M**. A representation theorem for **M** with respect to **B** would consist of the assertion that given any model

[7]An interesting example showing the usefulness of discussing the concept of reductionism and emergence in Suppes' terms can be found in Moulines (2006).

M in **M** there exists a model in **B** isomorphic to *M*. (Suppes 1988b, 259–260)

Once these models have been chosen and the isomorphism between them and the other models of the theory have been shown, it is then possible to work just on a subset of the models of the theory. The advantage consists in the fact that one can then work on a subset of these models, rather than on all of them, thus simplifying the task.

It is Suppes' deep conviction that the best insight into the structure of a complex theory is by seeking representation theorems for its models. The goal in analyzing a theory is thus

> [...] to discover if an interesting subset of models for the theory may be found such that any model for the theory is isomorphic to some member of this subset. To find such a distinguished subset of models for a theory and show that it has the property indicated is to prove a representation theorem for the theory. (Suppes 1967, 263)

In this way it is possible not only to restrict the discussion of some theoretical issues (such as reductionism) in the philosophy of science to a well-defined and rigorous framework, but also, while avoiding the excessive oversimplification of the first-order frameworks, to exploit all the useful mathematical tools both in the formulation of the theory and in the analysis of the structure of its models (Suppes 2002). This is clear in the example of the reduction in physics of thermodynamics to statistical mechanics; even if such reduction may be not satisfactory from a logical point of view, it nonetheless represents one of the great results of classical physics. In a sense, even though it was not possible to give a rigorous foundation to this reduction, physicists went on solving important mechanical problems under this assumption.

> Perhaps the most famous case to consider is the reduction of thermodynamics to statistical mechanics. [...] But Nagel fully realized he was not able to give the full details or to begin to offer a rigorous mathematical proof of an appropriate representation theorem. [...] And physicists, clever problem solvers that they are, have gone ahead and learned much about such phenomena, including how to calculate, without rigorous justification, a large number of quantitative results. (Suppes 2002, 467)

2.3.2 Representing through invariance

One of the main goals when representing a scientific theory (in the formal terms just discussed) is to detect its invariants, namely what remains constant under different conditions, for example, different units of measurements, different spatial positions for two observers of a moving figure. What these different conditions are will vary from one theory to another.

"Something is invariant if it is not varying, unalterable, unchanging, or constant" (Suppes 2001b, 1569). If we restrict ourselves to this rough definition, nothing seems to be invariant in our evolving universe. But, if we try to be a bit less naive and we take invariance as a relative concept, it is very easy to find examples of things that are invariant with respect to something else. For instance, the number of the ancestors of someone is invariant through time, while the number of his or her descendants is not. The structure of a building is invariant through a certain period of time, while the number of the people inside the building is probably not invariant in the same time slice.[8] The sentence expressing that Venus has a greater mass than Earth is true or false independently of the unit of measure used for the mass.

> The truth value of the statement is invariant under an arbitrary (positive) similarity transformation of the units of mass used in attempting to verify or falsify the statement. On the other hand the statement that the mass of Venus is greater than 1010 has no such invariance, for its truth or falsity will vary with the units of mass selected. (Suppes 1965, 365)

It is evident how different geometrical figures are invariant under different kinds of transformations. Good examples are two-dimensional figures: while the square is invariant under a limited number of rotations (90, 180, 270, 360 degrees), the circle is invariant under an infinite number of rotations.

In all these cases invariance concerns invariance of representation up to some set of transformations, e.g., changing measurements from feet to meters. How invariance is related to the explanation of scientific structures relies on the nature of representation. In order to axiomatize a theory, it is necessary not only to define its set-theoretical models and to prove representation theorems about the theory, but also to find the transformations under which the fundamental or primitive properties can vary to some important transformations. Such individuation means to seek the 'objective' meaning of a phenomenon, so that 'objective' is identified with 'invariant with respect to a given framework

---

[8]We owe this example to Suppes himself who mentioned it during an interview.

of reference'. It is just by singling out which are the things in a theory that are invariant (or constant) with respect to certain transformations that one can grasp the objective meaning of that theory.

In a sense, we could say that Suppes anchors his own notion of objectivity to that of invariance. In order to illustrate this point, he gives a couple of examples:

> Why is invariance important? One term that is used, that is a nice loaded philosophical term, is that it's only the invariants of a theory that are objective. The objective meaning is only given by the invariants. So, for example, in the case of special relativity it's the proper time that is the invariant, when the scales of measuring classical space and time are fixed, e.g. meters for space and seconds for time. The ordinary notion of distance between two points varies from one frame of reference to another, and so doesn't have an objective character, whereas the proper time does. Now, the proper time of course does have units. So we can say that the most austere Greek sense of invariance is found in the ratio of two proper times, which is a pure number. You can then axiomatize theories like mechanics. Newton's *Principia* (1687) is the last great physical treatise written in terms of ratios. What's important, I think, is not to have the axioms necessarily for complicated theories in terms of the invariants, but to recognize what the invariants are. So the theorems, in the same way as the axioms, must express some invariant property in order to be proper theorems. (Interview, 20 November 2003)

From this perspective the concept of invariance deals with that of meaningfulness (Suppes 1988b, 2001b). Let us consider geometry that, from a historical point of view, is one of the first domains in which the relation between invariance and meaningfulness has emerged. Taking Euclidian geometry as a simple example, we could say that the notion of orientation (up and down) is not meaningful in it, since it is not invariant under rotation, translation and reflection, the three invariant groups of motions. In other terms, if we are reasoning in the framework of Euclidian geometry, we do not know about orientation, as it is not preserved by the just mentioned groups of motions. But invariance with respect to a group of transformations is not the only possible notion of invariance. More strongly, invariance can be defined with respect to a theory, as the nature of these transformations is determined by the theory.

> As is emphasized in foundational discussions of classical physics, spatial and temporal intervals are observer-independent, but the concepts

of the center of the universe, the beginning of time or being in a state of absolute rest are not invariant and thus have no physical meaning, in spite of earlier views, such as those of Aristotelian physics, to the contrary. (Suppes 2001b, 1575)

If a representation theorem is devoted to identifying the fundamental properties of a theory and serves to isolate a significant subset among the models in order to work on such subset, the correlating invariance theorem states the uniqueness of a representation. The requirement of invariance, namely the degree of uniqueness of a scientific structure, emerges in the case of numerical representations and not in the case of purely qualitative relations.

It is when the concepts are given in terms of the representation, for example a numerical representation in the case of measurement, that the test for invariance is needed. When purely qualitative relations are given, which are defined in terms of the qualitative primitives of a theory, for example, those of Euclidean geometry, then it follows at once that the defined relations are invariant and therefore meaningful. On the other hand, the great importance of the representations is the reduction in computations and notation they achieve, as well as understanding of structure. This makes it imperative that we have a clear conception of invariance and meaningfulness for representations which may be, in appearance, rather far removed from the qualitative structures that constitute models of the theory. (Suppes 1988b, 267; 2002, 112)

At an operational level, invariance can be captured by solving the so called 'uniqueness problem', that is to say by finding the set of appropriate transformations under which a representation is invariant. These transformations must be expressed by a uniqueness theorem. The *uniqueness* theorem is sometimes called the *invariance* theorem:

Given a class of models, [...] with respect to which any other model of the theory can be represented, the invariance theorem is an expression of how unique is the representation in terms of such an analytic model. (Suppes 2001a, 1029)

In the theory of measurement, it is a natural question to ask, in the case of a measured property of an object, how the number used to measure this property is unique. "For example, the mass of a pebble may be measured in grams or pounds. The number assigned to measure mass is unique once a unit has been chosen" (Suppes 1988b, 264).

From an empirical point of view, the significance of the transformation characteristic of a quantity is the fact of expressing how unique is the structural isomorphism between the empirical operations adopted to obtain a given measurement and the corresponding arithmetical operations. In the case in which the empirical operation is simply that of ordering a group of objects according to some features, the corresponding arithmetical operation is that of less than (or greater than).

> An empirical hypothesis, or any statement in fact, which uses numerical quantities is empirically meaningful only if its truth value is invariant under the appropriate transformations of the numerical quantities involved. (Suppes 1988b, 265)

Any representation, in the formal sense advocated by Suppes, is incomplete without an accompanying study of invariance of representation. For this reason, "[...] a representation theorem should ordinarily be accompanied by a matching invariance theorem stating the degree to which a representation of a structure is unique" (Suppes 2002, 111).

Representation and uniqueness theorems are the technical counterparts of the general concepts of representation and invariance that constitute the two pillars of Suppes' formalization. The 'language' of representation and invariance is not present in ordinary scientific activities; this is especially true if we refer to a formal treatment (like the one Suppes provides). However, even if physicists do not think in terms of representation and invariance, for Suppes philosophers of science should do it when thinking about the foundations of scientific disciplines, in order to attain the rigor and the insight required by a formal approach.

3

Representing Theories

The representation of scientific theories constitutes the core of Suppes' philosophical work, but it is fair to say that they can be represented in many ways. Among them, set-theoretical axiomatization allows for a representation in form of structures in which essential features can emerge. Accordingly, the philosopher of science does not look at scientific disciplines from the outside and comments on the sociological, psychological or anthropological genesis of scientific practices but, rather, as an *insider*, who tries to extract from the actual practices the nucleus of the discipline or, in other terms, the basic properties of the objects the discipline has the purpose of inquiring. Suppes himself exemplifies this attitude in his professional practice: trained as a physicist and a philosopher of science, he strongly believes that the philosophical analysis of science must be detailed and anchored to scientific practice. Thus, he works in specific areas of competence, providing reflections that in most cases are very focused, always paying attention to avoid incautious generalizations. This way, Suppes exemplifies a new wave in the philosophy of science that must interact with the growing complexity of science.

In this chapter we aim at discussing Suppes' analysis of scientific theories in comparison both with the traditional view promoted by the Vienna Circle (*standard* or *syntactic view*) and with *structuralism* and the *semantic view*. The traditional sketch depicts Suppes as an opponent of the syntactic view and as the founder of the semantic view. This is true in general, but the aim of this chapter is to show that these connections are much more complex and multifaceted than what is usually recognized.

3.1 The linguistic perspective

The traditional view of scientific theories that Patrick Suppes encountered at the beginnings of his career in the 1950's is the one developed by the logical empiricist tradition. This traditional sketch, also known as the *syntactic view*, considers a scientific theory as composed of two parts: the first one is an *abstract logical calculus* and the second one consists of the *correspondence rules* to assign empirical content to the calculus. The abstractness of the calculus is due to the fact that it consists of the axioms or the postulates that are selected to express the core of the theory. Abstract means here that the theory is 'abstracted' from its full details and considered in its constitutive and essential parts. This calculus, moreover, is expressed with the language of logic: the calculus includes the vocabulary of logic and the primitive symbols of the theory, which can be both theoretical terms (like electrons) and concrete terms (like observable quantities). These theories are usually expressed in first-order logic or, to be more precise, are those whose axioms are expressed with the language of first-order logic.

It is worth noting that the commitment to first-order logic is not an ideological choice. According to this picture, first-order logic is just one amongst many of the formal languages that can be adopted in describing the abstract logical calculus which a scientific theory consists of. First-order logic actually results as the language used in most theories, and this is due both to historical and to practical reasons. This language is powerful enough to express a great deal of contents but, at the same time, it is simple enough to be used by most philosophers of science who, in many cases, prefer to avoid too many technicalities. However, it has to be kept in mind that theories with standard axiomatization, even if in most cases are expressed with first-order logic, can in principle adopt other languages as well.

So far we have clarified the terms 'logical' and 'abstract'. We discuss now the term 'calculus'. The use of the term 'calculus' is not without reasons. It immediately gives the idea that this part of the theory has to do with a kind of mechanical process, a relation of deducibility that holds between the sentences forming the theory. Accordingly, a theory can be seen as a network of sentences linked by the relation of deducibility. That means that for the syntactic view, an empirical theory is determined by the class of its valid sentences:

> [...] for the logical empiricist the right way to define an empirical theory

T was to define a set of axioms from which all the other sentences valid in T are logically derivable. (Wójcicki 1994, 127)

The abstract logical calculus by itself is not, of course, sufficient to define a complete scientific theory: without the correspondence rules capable of assigning empirical content to the calculus, the theory lacks what it is usually referred to as *interpretation*. So, in this context, to interpret means to assign specific content to the primitive and derived symbols of the calculus.

The application of the abstract calculus to reality, necessary for example to apply theories to empirical phenomena, is made possible by the correspondence rules that translate, in a symmetric way,[9] empirical and observable entities into descriptive terms of the theory. In other words, correspondence rules are what provide the interpretation for the axioms:

> [...] for the logical empiricist to interpret a theory T in order to make it applicable to empirical phenomena was to define how to use the principles of the theory in order to derive from them the right conclusions on the observable states of affairs. (Wójcicki 1994, 125)

As said, this traditional view has been called syntactic. This is due not just to the use of first-order logic to express the theory. This is an important choice but not essential to the task of describing theories. Rather, it is because the main orientation is of linguistic type: while studying scientific theories, the focus is on the sentences composing the theory, that are analyzed both by themselves and in the relation of deducibility holding among them.

This is also the reason why this same tradition has been addressed by Suppes as 'linguistic'. This term emphasizes the way in which the theory is developed and the fact that in a linguistic perspective, the language in which the theory is expressed becomes central. As Frederick Suppe points out:

> to say that something is a linguistic entity is to imply that changes in its linguistic features, including the formulation of its axiom system, produce a new entity. Thus on the Received View, change in the formulation of a theory is a change in theory. (Suppe 1989, 3)

---

[9]Of course the correspondence between theory and reality is not straightforward: many intermediate levels exist. Theories cannot be applied directly to reality and reality cannot be completely accounted for by a theory. For some details on this, see Subsection 2.2.2.

According to Suppes, this linguistic perspective has been overestimated in the tradition prior to him. The logical empiricist view emphasizes the centrality of language in accordance with the idea that philosophy consists primarily of an analysis of language. This has concretely resulted in the tendency of many philosophers to stress the syntactical aspect of the first part of the theory (logical calculus). Not that, even in these cases, the semantic aspect (correspondence rules) is absent; rather, it seems secondary with respect to the logical calculus that appears to constitute the core of the theory. It is probably for this reason that the correspondence between the calculus and its concrete interpretation has not been fully carried out and an adequate semantics for the formal calculus is often missing (Suppes 1967, 57). On the contrary, Suppes does not deny the importance of the language for every scientific theory, but he believes that the study of the structure of a theory is the best insight into the theory itself and in this respect language has not such a central role to play.

Given that the purpose of the standard view is to represent scientific theories in a rigorous way, the overall result is rather schematic. By emphasizing the syntactical aspect of theories and by adopting first-order logic, it can happen to leave out some technical details that in many cases contribute to shed light on the very nature of scientific theories. After all, as Suppes notices in many points, scientific theories are neither like nectarines nor like rational numbers (Suppes 1967, 55): they are not physical objects and, more importantly, they cannot be defined in any sharp and definite way.

3.1.1   Leaving the standard view

Suppes' account of scientific theories originates in contraposition with the linguistic account offered by the logical empiricists. His main concern regards the structure of a scientific theory and not the language used to express it. This way, Suppes' approach has been addressed as non-linguistic, in contraposition with the linguistic account advanced by the logical empiricists.

It is very important now to fully work out the differences between theories as linguistic entities and theories as non-linguistic entities. 'Linguistic' here means that a theory is a collection of sentences and that the language in which these sentences are expressed is fundamental. Changing the language in which the theory is expressed means changing the theory itself. According to this perspective, when one wants to analyze the relation of the theory with reality, he or she should count on the classical concepts of the philosophy of language, such as *truth* or *reference*: a theory is true if it corresponds to reality. This correspondence can be accomplished only when a reference from the terms of the theory to the objects in the world exists.

It is worth noting, moreover, that to support this view a relation between laws and reality is required and a level of commitment—even if weak—to a certain kind of realism arises. Theories are faithful descriptions of reality, reality exists and is external to us, and science can give an adequate account of it.

On the contrary, Suppes is rather cautious in committing to these general philosophical positions; his approach to scientific theories tends to remain neutral with respect to general philosophical topics. This is not to be read as an anti-engagement attitude toward philosophical questions but, rather, as an attempt to shift the focus of the philosophy of science toward more concrete problems. This shift to detailed issues reflects Suppes' deep conviction that it is just starting from these details that even the most general philosophical problems can be discussed.

It is not easy to find Suppes' explicit condemnation of more traditional positions. Rather, he prefers to let emerge his ideas from practice. The following words, thus, are particularly significant.

> I see I am in clear disagreement with Tom Kuhn as well. Maybe one of the problems is that I live mainly in the twentieth century—and not in an early century—in my thinking about science. I agree with Tom's remarks that we want to discuss and think about these various anecdotal methods of dealing with sleeping astronomers and left-handed observations and what have you; they are important in science. But what I consider methodologically important is that there also has been a very competent and a very deep-running theory developed for handling them, and that if one deals with more sophisticated science and not merely with simple-minded examples, then the importance of that theory comes very much into evidence. (Suppe 1977, 297)

The difficulty for a detailed characterization of scientific theories is one of the reasons why Suppes rejects the standard view in favor of a different approach: in considering the best way to express a theory, Suppes claims that first-order logic is not powerful enough to express the mathematical details of most scientific theories which he does not want to leave out. To give a more accurate account of scientific practice a different approach is needed. Suppes' choice is set theory: it provides operators extensively used in mathematics and so it is able to give reasons, at least partially, for the strong mathematical character of most scientific theories.

As Suppes points out (Suppes 1967, 57), philosophers often talk about theories in a simplified way which—for descriptive purposes— the traditional linguistic sketch based on first-order logic is enough for. However, first-order logic is not sufficient, in terms of expressive power, to fully represent theories. This does not imply a rejection of logic in its generality, but rather attempts to overcome its limits.

Suppes' solution is the extension of the framework of elementary logic by adding the axioms of set theory. This point requires further attention for basically two reasons: first, because Suppes' attitude toward first-order logic has often been misunderstood; second, because to fully grasp his approach to scientific theories, the understanding of the real motivations for moving in the direction of set theory is fundamental.

Let us consider the first reason: it may seem that Suppes rejects first-order logic in favor of set theory. First-order logic and set theory may be seen as alternative and antagonist ways of expressing scientific theories: the choice of one 'language' implies the rejection of the other. But this is not really the case. Suppes' position is neither a complete rejection nor a stretching out of the framework of basic logic. As Suppes himself points out, the mathematical character of scientific theories needs to be taken into account seriously and this can be done by means of set theory.

To further strengthen this point Suppes discusses some examples (Suppes 2002). One of these examples is particularly insightful. It is argued that, in mechanics, in order to formulate interesting problems[10], the elementary theory of real numbers is not sufficient. In particular, if one wants to deal with the solution of differential equations, standard mathematical analysis is required. However, to refute elementary logic (first-order logic) *in toto* is utterly impractical, since it works well to express the elementary parts of the theory. Neither would it be feasible to try to expand the framework of elementary logic to deal with

---

[10]Although Suppes does not specify what 'interesting' means here, it is likely that he is referring to theories complex enough to represent portions of the world in a sufficiently detailed way.

the additional body of mathematical concepts: that would require a strong effort with a quite unpractical result.

The difficulties of standard formalization[11] may lead us to believe that a rigorous account of scientific theories is not possible: this is absolutely not the case for Suppes. However, we need to spell out what exactly 'formal' means in this context and what solution can be adopted to overcome the limitations of first-order logic. Using Suppes' words:

> From a formal standpoint the essence of this approach is to add axioms of set-theory to the framework of elementary logic, and then to axiomatize scientific theories within this set-theoretical framework. (Suppes 2002, 30)

So elementary logic is maintained, but in the wider framework of set theory.

What is the motivation for moving toward set theory? A first immediate answer is that set theory is more expressive than first-order logic as a language in which to define mathematical concepts; plus, elementary logic and set theory together can offer a more sophisticated tool for representing theories. But, still, this does not explain why set theory specifically—and no other choices—can successfully expand the traditional framework. The core issue here is to answer how set theory can account for the mathematical background of most scientific theories. It is quite surprising to observe that Suppes, in an interview, (Interview, 24 October 2002) emphasizes that what really matters within set theory is the primitive binary relation of membership. It is exactly membership that gives variable levels, impossible to have with first-order logic, and allows for building a hierarchy: set theory offers the tools to express that the variable x is included in the set a which is included, in turn, in the set consisting of the sets a and b. In practice, this means to admit that any set-theoretical predicate can be expressed exclusively in terms of membership.

> Yet one of the great triumphs from a conceptual standpoint in mathematics, especially the foundations of mathematics over the last hundred years, has been to show precisely how such a reduction could be made in completely explicit and rigorous terms. It is, it seems to me, one of the great intellectual surprises about the structure of mathematics that

---

[11] By standard formalization we mean here the one using only first-order logic in the representation of scientific theories.

the standard mathematical notions can be reduced by explicit definition just to the simple concept of set membership. (Suppes 1972, 12)

3.1.2 Different directions, but same tradition

A comparison between Suppes and the syntactic view cannot omit, despite the macroscopic differences just pointed out, to note that Suppes' philosophy of science belongs to the same tradition of the logical empiricists. By saying that, we do not want to deny the differences between the two. However, both Suppes and the logical empiricists share a strong conviction: they believe that philosophy, and philosophy of science in particular, should use a fully precise language and acquire a rigorous approach in dealing with the explanation of scientific theories (Wójcicki 1994, 129).

Therefore, in both cases a formal approach is advocated. A first difference concerns the framework in which this enterprise is carried out. According to the syntactic view, formality is achieved by the extensive application of first-order logic playing a clarifying role for philosophy, whereas Suppes introduces set theory to overcome the limitations of formal logic. The second difference regards the range of applicability of formal methods. Contrary to the logical empiricists, Suppes does not aim to apply his formal approach to the whole science, but just to the foundational issues of specific scientific disciplines, like, for instance, physics or probability theory. Moreover, logical empiricists tend to reject informal methods in philosophy, calling for an approach as formal as possible, Suppes is instead fully aware that informal methods are the necessary complement of even the most rigorous accounts of science (see also Chapter 5).

In this comparison, it is interesting to note the existence of a line of continuity between the logical empiricists' tradition and Suppes' approach also from a strictly historical point of view. This continuity is represented by Ernest Nagel, who was Suppes' mentor and one of the most influential figures on his education. In his *Intellectual Autobiography* (Suppes 1979b, 5) Suppes recognizes Nagel's influence over all the other ones. Nagel's skeptical, detailed, and patient philosophical analyses are remembered by Suppes as essential in the formation of his philosophical skills. It is not by chance that, at the same time, Nagel was in strong connection with Rudolf Carnap, one of the philosophers who diffused the logical empiricism's tradition in the United States.

3.2 Models and structures

In order to overcome the linguistic characterization of theories, Suppes analyzes the latter starting from their structure. A theory is something clearly different from its formulation in a particular language. So there is not as much interest in how the theory is formulated; the only important question concerns its structure. Therefore, how the theory is presented by the language can be largely ignored (van Fraassen 1989).

One of the ways of analyzing the structure of a scientific theory is to define the intended class of models of the theory. As Suppes writes: "To ask if we can axiomatize the theory is then just to ask if we can state a set of axioms such that the models of these axioms are precisely the models in the defined class" (Suppes 2002, 5). Now, it seems clear that, according to Suppes, if we want to put our attention on the structure of the theory, we need to analyze the structure of the models of the theory. However, this passage requires further attention since it is central for understanding the answer Suppes proposes to respond to the central question 'What is a scientific theory?'. Exactly, what does it mean to analyze the structure of a scientific theory in terms of its models?

In the contraposition between syntactic/standard view, from the one side, and Suppes' view, from the other one, Suppes himself introduces a further distinction, that of *intrinsic* versus *extrinsic* characterization of theories (Suppes 1967, 2002). Extrinsic here refers to the perspective for which theories are regarded from 'outside' a particular logical and linguistic formulation and, hence, the emphasis is put on the structure of the theory. He argues that a theory with standard formalization, by emphasizing the linguistic aspect, provides an intrinsic characterization, whereas to give an extrinsic characterization it is sufficient to define the class of the models of the theory. Following this line of argument it seems natural the identification of intrinsic with syntactic and of extrinsic with semantic, where semantic is intended in the sense of dealing with models. However, the point here is deeper: Suppes does not state that in the syntactic view models are out of the question (and in the following it will become clear how models can be introduced even in the syntactic framework). He argues, instead, that in the syntactic view an explicit consideration of models is lacking, even if this could offer an insight into the nature of scientific theories.

It is precisely by explicit consideration of the class of models of the theory that the problem can be put into proper perspective and formulated in a fashion that makes possible consideration of its exact solution. [...] We can view the tacit assumption of a frame of reference as an extrinsic aspect of the familiar characterizations of the theory. (Suppes 1967, 61)

There are other ways to put this distinction: the extrinsic characterization is usually given via numerical representations, while the intrinsic via qualitative notions; furthermore, in the extrinsic characterization notions used in the axiomatization are not invariant with respect to the main transformations of the theory, while in the intrinsic characterization invariant notions are preferred. As an example, one can take geometry, where an extrinsic characterization can be given by measurement's units, like meters and yards, while an intrinsic characterization may be given by points, lines, surfaces etc.

Let's start with an example from geometry: so, if we treat geometry as analytic geometry, that would be an extrinsic characterization, and we would write down the axioms we needed and they would just be numerical in character, about the coordinates and angles etc., and so that would be all numerical in spirit and then we could talk about angles in terms of cosine measurements etc. and so we can extrinsically talk about having an axiomatization of the geometry. [...] Now, the intrinsic way: we start with some qualitative notions; for example, if we want to do Euclidean geometry, we can take betweenness, which will give us an affine characterization, we can do an affine space just in terms of betweenness, and then we add to that congruence of segments. So, those are the only two notions and we have qualitative axioms in terms of those two notions. Now, the problem is to know when are the axioms satisfactory? Well, the Greeks had more problems about that than we do, for we have an extrinsic characterization. We want to prove a representation theorem that any model of the qualitative axioms using these two primitive notions is isomorphic to the standard analytical geometric three-dimensional Euclidean model. So we have both an intrinsic characterization for which we can prove such a theorem and we have the fixed analytic model.

Now, in mechanics (let's take a more complicated example, but it's important not to just have geometry). The ordinary axioms are given extrinsically, because you use notions in the axioms that are not invariant under, say, classical mechanics' Galilean transformations or relativistic mechanics' Lorentz transformations. So, we talk about the ordinary coordinates' system and we're really measuring things with respect to the laboratory at rest. Those measurements in themselves aren't invariant. So, if we use another laboratory that's in a spatial [...] satellite, then we'll have different measurements. So, we could axiomatize just in terms of intrinsic measurements, we might have to decide how to construct them, but now the axioms are not qualitative, but they are intrinsic in the sense that the only notions used in the axioms are invariant notions, i.e., notions that are invariant under the Galilean transformations or Lorentz transformations. (Interview, 20 November 2003)

To choose to characterize a theory in terms of its models means to focus on the structure of the theory itself and to consider the structure predominant with respect to the language in which the theory is expressed. In particular, Suppes strongly believes that "the best insight into the structure of a complex theory is by seeking representation theorems for its models" (Suppes 1988b, 254) and that "the explicit consideration of models can lead to a more subtle discussion of the nature of a scientific theory" (Suppes 2002, 6). Our aim in the rest of this chapter is to clarify why.

3.2.1   Models as 'the thing depicted'

First of all the term "model" has to be intended in the logical sense (see Chapter 2 for further details); accordingly, the model is the thing depicted by a theory. For example, instead of saying that certain equations are a model of subatomic phenomena (as happens in the empirical sciences), Suppes (together with all the logicians and mathematicians adopting this definition) says that the subatomic phenomena are models of the theory represented by these equations.

As it has been noted by Balzer et al. (1987) this use of model in the sense of 'the thing depicted' is not restricted to logic or mathematics, but appears also in ordinary language. This is the case when one says that a person is the model of a painting: the model is the person depicted and the painting is the picture of him or her.

Following this view and trying to be more specific on the notion of model, it is possible to say that a model is a structure consisting of a domain of entities and some relations defined over them that satisfy certain conditions. The way in which a theory can be associated with a homogeneous class of models may deeply vary (see for example the *Proceedings of the 2004 Biennial Meeting of The Philosophy of Science Association Part II* in (Solomon 2007)); however, according to this view, there is always a definite class of models uniquely associated with a given theory (Moulines 2006).

The shifting of the attention from language to models is one of the most original features in Suppes' account of scientific theories. Suppes is probably the first philosopher to assign the concept of model a key role in the philosophy of science. In the picture of scientific theory seen as a calculus with correspondence rules, no space is left for introducing models as a way of characterizing theories. The concept of model has been deliberately left out from the philosophical and scientific analysis because of the conviction that it lacks the sharpness to allow for multiple representations of the same phenomena (think for example of Carl Hempel (1965) or Rudolf Carnap (1939)).

The emphasis on logic as a way to clarify the essence of theories is accompanied in the logical empiricists with the refusal to acknowledge a possible role for models in science. It is worth stressing that in these contexts the concept of model is generically defined and it is probably not intended in the strong mathematical sense Suppes proposes. Therefore, the role of models in scientific reconstruction is almost completely denied. Models are just weakened pictures of phenomena, that are far distant from the type of pictures returned by scientific theories.

To mention one specific position, it is interesting to refer to Rudolf Carnap. He introduces the concept of model in *Foundations of Logic and Mathematics* in the *International Encyclopedia of Unified Science* when speaking of the development of physics and its formalization, intended as the construction of a calculus supplemented by an interpretation. A model is used when non intuitive formulas (e.g. Maxwell's equations of electromagnetism) are proposed as new axioms. In this case a model is a way of representing electromagnetic processes by analogy to already known processes, like movements of visible things. However, Carnap declares that this direction is not satisfactory and affirms:

> It is important to realize that the discovery of a model has no more than an aesthetic or didactic or at best a heuristic value, but is not at all essential for a successful application of the physical theory. (Carnap 1939, 69)

It is clear now that the choice of characterizing theories in terms of their models is not just a matter of formalisms (first-order logic versus set theory), but of the kind of object a theory is considered to be. The use of set theory (or better, the use of elementary logic expanded with the axioms of set theory) to represent scientific theories is not an 'ideological' choice: set theory is acknowledged only as the best means of expression to render the mathematical character of most scientific theories. To consider a theory as determined by the class of its models is a very precise choice that really moves Suppes' view of theories away from the logical positivism. It is the choice of seeing scientific theories from a well defined perspective, opposed to that lying beneath theories as logical calculi:

> To think of a theory as a network of sentences linked by the relation of deducibility or to think of it as a set of claims that concern a specific class of structures is to choose between two dramatically different perspectives. (Wójcicki 1994, 127)

Not that the consideration of models is completely lacking in the syntactic view. The difference is, again, in the focus. In the syntactic view, the focus is on syntax, namely on the fact that theories are described and expressed by means of words or sentences and models are the interpretation of an abstract logical calculus. On the contrary Suppes, by expressing scientific theories purely in terms of models, exploits models as non-linguistic entities in which theories are satisfied, rather than as descriptions. In Suppes' words:

> It is very widespread practice in mathematical statistics and in the behavioral sciences to use the word *model* to mean the set of quantitative assumptions of the theory, that is, the set of sentences which in a precise treatment would be taken as axioms or, if they are themselves not explicit enough, would constitute the intuitive basis for formulating a set of axioms. (Suppes 2002, 20)

In both cases (models as descriptions and models as non-linguistic entities) axiomatization is the starting point: to say that a theory is axiomatically built means that the set of valid sentences of the theory is defined as a set of given axioms of the theory together with their logical consequences. The difference lies in the kind of framework this axiomatization is included in: it can be either a linguistic framework (as in the logical empiricism) or a set-theoretical framework (as in Suppes' view).

The important point that has to be grasped in order to understand the difference between the syntactic view and Suppes' view is that the latter is not only a matter of the language used, but it is also a matter of the perspective adopted to shed light on theories: to put it clearly, Suppes' perspective is shaped by set theory and by the use of models.

In Suppes' approach any theory is determined by the class of its possible realizations and not by the group of its valid sentences. Accordingly, even the relationship between theory and reality should be revised in this direction. Now, models (and not correspondence rules) provide the interpretation for the axioms; hence the passage from theory to reality is not direct but is mediated by models. The philosopher of science does not need anymore to look for a correspondence between what the theory says and how the world is in order to evaluate the adequacy of a scientific theory. Now, since any theory requires an interpretation in order not to remain just a formal system, this interpretation is a much more complex process but, at the same time, it offers the nuances able to depict a more sophisticated way in which a theory may *represent* reality. Here the idea is to start from the beginning with the possible realizations of a theory, that is to say that interpretation is not a second step, but it is already included in the characterization of a scientific theory. Theories are not just empty forms, but structures already accompanied by interpretation.

3.2.2 Between structuralism and the semantic view

To fully grasp the general viewpoint of Suppes' approach it may be interesting to ask the role of set-theoretical predicates in relation to scientific theories. For this purpose Suppes adopts the notion of *structure*, that can be understood more intuitively than that of set-theoretical predicate. More precisely, set-theoretical predicates are used to specify classes of structures (Suppes 2002, 33); thus, a theory is a set of claims that concern a specific class of structures, and the transformations under which that class is invariant. So structures characterize a theory and help us to identify its basic elements.

The emphasis on structures connects Suppes with the approach adopted by a group of mathematicians of the last century, better known as *Bourbaki*. Nicolas Bourbaki is not the name of a single mathematician, but of a group of, mainly French, mathematicians. The group was founded in 1935 and is still working, even if it has been active especially from 1950 to 1970. What is much more important about the Bourbaki program is the identification of basic structures and their role in many different parts of mathematics. A group, for example, is an abstract structure defined by means of a number of axioms. This abstract structure can have several concrete realizations, such as the set of real numbers with the addition operation. Suppes himself acknowledges (2002, 33) the similarity of his approach with Bourbaki's. But while recognizing that Bourbaki's program is entirely committed to mathematics, he is interested in the basic structures of empirical sciences as well. Even though at the end Suppes' subscription to this approach is only partial:

> There's an element of abstraction or generality I think that pedagogically is difficult for students for instance and I believe intuitively in a more genetic approach, even if you end up with very formal definitions, but Bourbaki has written in a very austere and rigorous way and I think not the best for teaching anything to students or even maybe thinking about it yourself. (Interview, 20 November 2003)

There is also another sense of structuralism that originates from Suppes' approach and presents many analogies with it. Its most known representatives are Sneed (1971), Stegmuller (1979), and Balzer et al. (1987). In this case there exists a much stronger connection with Suppes' work, since many of the founders of this structuralist program have been in deep contact with Suppes himself and his work. Also in this case the Bourbaki's concept of *species of structures*[12] plays a central role in the axiomatization of a scientific theory. However, structuralism here is not just a mathematical approach, but tries to expand further on other scientific disciplines, first of all physics. The almost exclusive use of set-theoretical tools, as opposed to linguistic analysis, shows the relevant debt to Suppes' approach. At the same time, this structuralist program goes on in the process of discussing problems, such as reduction of a theory to another one or incommensurability, on an almost completely formal level, focussing on the problem of characterizing the theoretical concepts as opposed to the empirical ones.

The strong connections between Suppes and the structuralists mentioned above are undeniable. But in a sense, the structuralist program as presented by Sneed (1971) in his seminal book is more ambitious than Suppes' one: he presents a meta-theory of the whole physics in

---

[12]A species of structures is a set that typically characterizes the general species to which the structure belongs, where a structure is now defined by characterizing some of the members of this set by means of an axiom of the species of structure (Bourbaki 2004).

the model-theoretic tradition launched by Suppes. However, the formal apparatus developed to achieve the goal can be easily subjected to the following criticism: is it worth constructing this weighty formal apparatus just to describe the domain in question and to solve specific problems? More: to what extent is this formal framework really necessary to achieve these goals? Suppes himself, being in general very sympathetic with the structuralist account, advances some perplexities on the very general philosophical ground lying beneath Sneed's program in particular. His words are illuminating both in motivating his doubts and in presenting his view:

> My view of science has moved increasingly from that of a foundationalist to the viewpoint that the conceptual content of science is best analyzed in terms of a diverse set of methods for solving a wide variety of problems. Schemes of great generality about scientific explanation, such as those of Sneed, can perhaps be useful in providing some kind of general framework, but I think they miss the main part of what we intuitively want from good scientific explanations. Moreover, our sense of satisfaction with good explanations is particularistic in nature and not in any natural way subsumed under the general schema proposed by Joe [Sneed].[. . .] It is only a myth engendered by philosophers—even in the past to some extent by myself—that the deductive organization of physics in nice set-theoretical form is an achievable goal. A look at the chaos in the current literature in any part of physics is enough to quickly dispel that illusion. This does not mean that set-theoretical work cannot be done, it is just that its severe limitations must be recognized. (Suppes 1994, 213)

This long quotation shows very well Suppes' commitment to the set-theoretical approach but, at the same time, the realistic evaluation of its limits. His skepticism in the success of the general schemes represents a further critique of some traditional philosophy of science in search of universal frameworks.

Besides the structuralist stance, the approach developed by Suppes starting from the second half of the last century is often referred to as the *semantic view* to stress its contraposition with the syntactic view. The term 'semantic' puts the emphasis on meaning rather than on syntax that, in seeing theories as logical calculi, is instead prevalent. This semantic conception derives its name "from the fact that it construes theories as what their formulations refer to when the formulations are given a (formal) *semantic* interpretation" (Suppe 1989, 4). Semantic is used in this context in the sense of formal semantics of mathematical logic.

Suppes is considered the father of the semantic view of theories. According to the semantic view, to present a theory is to present a family of models. This presupposes the abandonment of the linguistic approach and implies a structuralist position. Let us consider the first claim: according to Suppes, the language in which the theory is expressed is not fundamental; to change this language does not mean to change the theory. This is strictly connected with a structuralist stance and with the second claim above: the core of a theory is its structure, namely what remains invariant under some group of transformations. The family of models presented by a scientific theory are mathematical structures. In the realm of mathematics isomorphic objects are not relevantly different; this is the reason why mathematical objects are referred to as structures. If the models used to represent scientific theories are mathematical objects, therefore scientific theoretical descriptions are structural.

The semantic approach could be seen as including the structuralism considered above. For some, the semantic view is the current form of the general idea of structuralism (van Fraassen 1997). What changes in the different versions of the semantic view is the characterization of the structures constituting the core of a scientific theory. For Suppes and some structuralists, theories are characterized as set-theoretical predicates, for others (e.g. Beth and van Fraaseen) they are state spaces, for others again they are relational systems. On the contrary, some others stress the differences, rather than the similarities, in the treatment of theories between the more general semantic view and the structuralist approach (Suppe 1977). We are not interested in this distinction here, but just in understanding how the semantic conception of theories has originated from Suppes' view of theories as set-theoretical models.

The semantic view assumes many varieties in the philosophy of science (Psillos 2006). It can have a methodological interest, claiming that theories are best understood in terms of models; it can be an epistemic approach for which structure is what can be best understood; it can assume the form of an ontic position, for which there is nothing without structure. Suppes has not taken a definite position on these different varieties, but probably the best characterization of his approach is in methodological terms, even with all the limitations highlighted above.

To say that to present a theory is to present a class of models (van Fraassen 1997), or that a theory is something uniquely associated with a homogeneous class of models (Moulines 2006), or that a theory is defined as a class of models (Suppe 1977) is clearly very different. Again, we are not interested here in distinguishing these differences and in analyzing the philosophical commitments behind them. We are interested, rather, in underlining the common features of the semantic view. Even if most of the proponents of this view have recognized that there is more than structure in a scientific theory, the structural analysis remains the fundamental support of any reflection about scientific theories. Theories defined in terms of models, such as the full recognition of the role of models (regardless of their nature) in characterizing scientific theories, remain at the core of the semantic view, in spite of all the current debate about the limits of an account in terms of models. And without doubt, Suppes is at the origin of this approach.

While recognizing Suppes' approach at the core of the semantic view, we observe as well a fundamental difference between Suppes and the current semantic view on theories. Within the semantic approach, models have become the privileged entities to characterize a scientific theory. Moreover, starting from this characterization, the semantic view has emphasized the attention on the way in which theories are used in scientific practice,[13] in contrast with the simplified reconstruction of theories promoted by the syntactic view. One of the virtues of the semantic conception is the aim of reflecting the practice of actual science. Instead of constructing a first-order axiomatizable language for, say, a theory in physics and then proposing various rules of interpretation, one can directly define the class of models that are the subject matter of the theory.

But this centrality of models has resulted in a 'totality' of models: in others words, it seems that the explanation in terms of models can exhaust any level of analysis, from foundational issues to problems of use. In some cases the semantic conception prescribes that theories have to be totally identified with their models. A claim that cannot be accepted by many. This is also the reason why, in the last years, even some philosophers working in the semantic view have turned

---

[13]See more on this in Chapter 5.

from the idea that just models count and moved towards the recovery of theories (Morrison 2007), of syntactic elements as descriptions (Mattingly 2005), or of representations (Frigg 2006), recognizing that models cannot be the only reliable elements in the explanation of science.

Regarding this problem, Suppes has always been very clear in establishing the role of models, and their limits, within philosophy of science. He believes that speaking in terms of models, and in particular set-theoretical models, is the best way for speaking of the foundations of scientific theories. However, he is not interested in the ways models function in the acquisition of scientific knowledge. This is because physicists do not think in terms of models when they work on their problems and so to force the scientific practice into an explanation in terms of models is too restrictive. When using a scientific theory, one may pay very little attention to the models of the theory. From a practical point of view theories are not seen in terms of models. This is important, instead, within philosophy of science, where one of the aims is to clarify scientific theories from a foundational point of view.

Accordingly, the first concern of philosophers of science ought to be with the exact specification of theoretical structures, rather than with analyzing how models are used by scientists in their actual problems. This way, Suppes easily avoids the critique moved to the most recent semantic conceptions almost entirely focussed on models, not just for foundational purposes, but also to try to understand the scientific practice. Suppes's set-theoretical formalization in terms of models covers a well defined field, namely that of the foundations of specific scientific disciplines. For example Suppes' semantic conception is at its best as a theory of measurement where he illustrates how mathematics can be applied to real-world systems. This detailed analysis in terms of set-theoretical models gets more complicated in other cases (see Chapter 5). For this reason Suppes is constantly aware of the limits of such formalization. The ontic commitments of science at work may be different than the ontic commitments of the philosophy of science (Suppe 1989). A difference to be also accounted for reflecting on the deep meaning of Suppes' formalization and its limits, which are the object of the next chapter.

4

The Meaning of Formalization

Despite Suppes' emphasis on formalization, it would be misleading to present his position as a 'formalizing program'. This is because one of the distinctive traits of his philosophy is a pluralistic attitude and he himself has always refused general characterizations of his work. The refusal of a unifying view probably derives from the vastness and diversity of Suppes' interests: he knows very well that current science is complex and that to describe it univocally would be unrealistic. However, despite this pragmatic pluralism, we deem that Suppes has promoted a method of analysis able to unify the richness and variety of science. The idea of 'unification' in this context needs to be handled with particular care: this is the reason why we prefer to speak of a *unifying method*, rather than a unifying view. This method represents a distinctive trait in Suppes' philosophy of science and, in this chapter, we discuss it by presenting its main features. We reflect on the sense of Suppes' formalization, by describing its nature, its context of applicability, and its historical roots as well. We start discussing the *focus* of formal methods on scientific theories by first analyzing the centrality of the formal approach in Suppes' philosophy; then, we consider the development of this approach and its *historical* and *conceptual roots*; finally, we present its context of *applicability* and its *limits*.

4.1 The centrality of formal methods

In this section we analyze our choice of formal methods as the unifying approach in Suppes' philosophy in comparison with other themes of his work. Then we present the focus of Suppes' formal approach, namely scientific theories, and how they can be formalized according to Suppes' proposal.

4.1.1 Why formalization?

Before analyzing in details what formalization exactly means for Suppes, we aim at justifying the centrality of formal methods in comparison with other Suppes' philosophical interests. Probability and probabilistic methods, in particular, constitute a central part of his work and, in many cases, they seem to represent 'the' unifying view. For example, in the introduction of the most extended and comprehensive collection of reflections on Suppes' philosophy, Paul Humphreys comments:

> Despite the catholicity of Suppes's interests, there is an underlying cohesiveness to his thought, due in large part to the methods he has developed and deployed over his career. One continuous thread running through Suppes's work has been an emphasis on the importance of probability and probabilistic theories. (Humphreys 1994, xii)

Or, to quote another contribution in the same book describing Suppes' philosophy of science as *probabilistic empiricism*:

> Probabilistic empiricism should then replace logical empiricism, and accordingly probability, and not logic, should be the point of departure of our investigation into philosophy of science and epistemology. (Galavotti 1994, 246)

Given what was just quoted, why emphasize formal methods as a unifying approach, instead of, for instance, probabilistic methods? The answer lies in the possibility, when using formal methods, to include probability as well as Suppes' empirical attitude in the same framework. In our opinion, formal methods represent a line of thought underlying several aspects of Suppes' philosophical work, including probability and probabilistic methods. One of our goals is to evaluate the methodological relevance of some ideas, such as formalization, within the scenario of a completely new vision of science and of philosophy of science.

Let us consider the case of probability: it is certainly true that probability plays a central role in Suppes' philosophy, Suppes himself declaring "I count probability as perhaps the single most important concept in the philosophy of science" (Suppes 2002, 14). However, even the treatment of probability is carried out in the framework of formal methods or, to be more precise, axiomatized in set-theoretical terms. Chapter 5 of Suppes (2002) opens with an axiomatization of probability that proceeds by defining the set-theoretical predicate 'is a probability space'. The purpose of the chapter is to set forth the standard axioms and concepts of probability theory in order to study the foundations of probability in the rest of the chapter.

Accordingly, we argue that formal methods offer a general and unifying view of Suppes' work as a philosopher of science. While recognizing the importance of this conceptual grinder, we acknowledge its coarseness as well: the richness of real science, of real scientific theories, cannot be wholly described in this account. The Suppesian image of science can reflect all its shadows without abandoning Suppes' desire for conceptual clarity. This granted, we do not argue in favor of formal methods as covering all aspects of Suppes' work as an empirical philosopher; rather we claim that the formal approach can be regarded as a way of recognizing a unifying method, even when this formality is achieved *a posteriori* as a way to clarify the foundations of a single scientific discipline or parts of it.

We are aware that, despite the unifying method constituting the core of Suppes' program in formalizing philosophy, it is not possible to summarize under just one heading what Suppes has produced in a very long career. Hence, we emphasize that the reference to a sort of unification does not mean here a monolithic characterization of Suppes' philosophy of science, but rather a methodological attitude that can be tracked in Suppes' production. To fully grasp how formal methods are applied by Suppes in the philosophy of science, let us start to explain the focus of Suppes' analysis, namely scientific theories.

4.1.2 Scientific theories

It is not common in Suppes' works to find a general analysis of science. Rather than wide characterizations of science, he usually prefers detailed and well circumscribed discussions of specific problems. A partial[14] exception is represented by the book *Representation and Invariance of Scientific Structures* (Suppes 2002) that, while collecting Suppes' main contributions to different parts of science, presents a comprehensive approach to the philosophy of science as well. As for Suppes it is

---

[14]We use the term 'partial' here since the book we are referring to does not abandon detailed analysis of specific fields even if, at the same time, it depicts some general lines of Suppes' thoughts.

highly difficult to simply characterize science, philosophy of science should accordingly reflect the plurality of science, both in terms of its topics and in terms of its methods.

The core questions for the philosophy of science are what science is and how it works. In Suppes' opinion, the best way to answer these questions is to focus on *scientific theories* considered as the basic unit of analysis (Suppes 2002, 2). It is indeed the analysis of scientific theories that is carried out within the formal framework that represents the strongest characterization of Suppes' approach to the philosophy of science. Formal methods function as a fixed frame of reference to discuss in a systematic way some of the issues emerging in the philosophy of science.

Taking scientific theories as the starting point of Suppes' philosophical analysis of science, it is not surprising that the title of a Suppes' famous paper is "What is a scientific theory?" (Suppes 1967). This paper opens by describing the standard[15] sketch (also called *syntactic view*) of scientific theories as formed by an abstract logical calculus (expressed using first-order logic) and a set of correspondence rules to assign empirical content to the calculus. A theory is a class of statements or propositions to be interpreted by the correspondence rules. According to Suppes (see Chapter 2), this characterization of scientific theories presents several problems. The main one is that it is too schematic and unrealistic. It is highly improbable to find in practice an example of a scientific theory in the form of a logical calculus composed of axioms and their logical consequences, except in very special cases.

Even if the main target point of Suppes' critique is the syntactic view, in the same paper, as well as in the 2002 book (Suppes 2002), he also discusses other views of scientific theories and, in particular, the *instrumental view*. According to the latter, theories are to be seen as *principles of inference*, from which it is possible to derive knowledge about facts. The focus is not on their truth or falsity, but on their ability to infer new facts. So *actions*, and not statements, represent the core of the theory. When actions occupy the central stage, it is evident that truth is not concerned and it is replaced by the concept of *expected*

---

[15]It is to be noted that 'standard' refers here to the view on scientific theories still largely diffused in the 1950's and 1960's, which Suppes reacts to at the beginning of his philosophical career.

loss or *risk*. Also, the instrumental view of theories can be treated formally, as has been done in modern statistical decision theory. In this case it presents a number of interesting and promising ideas capable, at least potentially, to overcome the schematism of the syntactic view. However, for Suppes, it is almost impossible to find ideas of statistical decision theory applied to concrete examples of complex scientific theories. In practice, even the decision theorists still find it more useful and natural to talk about semantic concepts, like that of truth (Suppes 1967).

What Suppes proposes, as alternative to the syntactic and other views, is an approach based on the concept of model (see Chapter 2). A theory is to be viewed as a *class* of models, instead of a set of sentences. A model is intended here as a *set-theoretical model*, namely "a structure consisting of some domains of entities and some relations defined over them and satisfying certain conditions" (Moulines 2006, 317). In other words, a *model* is a *possible realization* in which the theory is satisfied, where a possible realization is, according to Suppes, a *set-theoretical entity*. More precisely, a set-theoretical model is a certain kind of ordered tuple that consists of a set of objects and relations and operations on these objects (Suppes 2002).

As seen in Chapter 3, there are several reasons involved in the shifting from theories as logical calculi to models of theories. In general Suppes believes that "[...] it is pertinent and natural from a logical standpoint to talk about the models of the theory" (Suppes 1967, 57; 2002, 3) or that:

> [...] it is very much simpler to assert things about models of the theory rather than talk directly and explicitly about the sentences of the theory, perhaps the main reason for this being that the notion of a sentence of the theory is not well defined when the theory is not given in standard formalization. (Suppes 1967, 58)

At a first sight, the reason for introducing models to characterize theories could appear to be only a matter of adopting a different formalization. Set theory provides a more adequate framework to talk about science compared with elementary logic, which is too schematic for expressing the mathematical details of many scientific theories. However, the reason to introduce the concept of model to characterize scientific theories is deeper and concerns the idea of an adequate representation of scientific theories. The adequate representation of a theory is the one carried out in terms of its models. As seen in Chapter 3, this entails a different perspective on the representation of scientific theories.

An important consequence of focussing on models of theories is to put more attention to *real* scientific theories and how they *really* work. The result is to quit the rigid difference between theoretical terms and observational terms fostered by many traditional approaches to the philosophy of science. Instead, in Suppes' framework, the formal part of the theory should be accompanied by an empirical interpretation and this requires a way to relate theory to data. Experimentation needs as well to be considered a part of the theory, such as the statistical methodology for testing the theory itself. This amounts to introducing a whole hierarchy of theories to give reason, even from a formal point of view, of both the theoretical part and the experimental part, that together characterize scientific theories.

4.2 Formal methods in Suppes' philosophy

Since this chapter is a reflection on Suppes' approach to philosophy in order to elucidate the sense of his formalization, in this section we summarize the main traits of his methodology, already presented in more details in Chapter 2.

4.2.1 Set-theoretical axiomatization

The sense of Suppes' formalization may be expressed by two key-words: *axiomatization* and *set theory*. To adopt a formal approach in the philosophy of science means to axiomatize scientific theories in a certain manner. Axiomatization is a way of representing a scientific theory, dealing with the elucidation of its core parts. Axiomatization, hence, is the first feature of Suppes' formal approach and distinguishes it from other formal methods, such as *procedural approaches* characteristic of computer science and devoted to calculation (Suppes 1979a). On the other hand, axiomatization is common also to other formal approaches, such as the one advocated by the standard view, using first-order logic. What is different in Suppes' approach is the framework in which this axiomatization takes place. For a number of reasons[16] Suppes believes set theory is the most adequate scenario in which to axiomatize scientific theories. The famous Suppes' slogan 'to

---

[16]See Chapters 2 and 3 for a detailed discussion on this.

axiomatize a scientific theory is to define a set-theoretical predicate' programmatically states this style of axiomatization.

How does the axiomatization process work in the framework provided by set theory? According to Suppes (1954) this results in a four-step process.[17] First of all, it is necessary to clarify the theories, other than set theory, needed in carrying out the axiomatization process. This depends on the particular scientific theory which is under axiomatization. Second, the fundamental and primitive notions of the theory have to be indicated together with their set-theoretical features. This means, while axiomatizing, to have set theory in mind in order to choose the primitives which are the most appropriate to express axiomatization. Third, besides listing the axioms which must be satisfied, it is time to exploit the advantages of such a formal setting of axiomatization, such as to state the representation theorems that can be proved. This is particularly useful to set isomorphism about models representing different scientific theories and to analyze their properties. Models provide the connection between a theory and the phenomena under investigation through the notion of structure. More precisely, the notion of model makes the idea of *same structure* precise through the concept of *isomorphism*. Finding an isomorphism among models implies that it is possible to infer facts about an empirical model isomorphic to a theoretical one. Fourth, the axiomatized theory needs to be interpreted, that means to indicate how to satisfy the axioms representing the theory.

That said, it is not surprising that the title of the book collecting Suppes' lifetime work is *Representation and Invariance of Scientific Structures*. As already explained in Chapter 2, for Suppes the first step in characterizing a theory is to provide a *representation* of it. The representation of a scientific theory is thus given in terms of its models, more precisely models expressed in a set-theoretical framework. Representation is carried out by means of an axiomatization in set-theoretical terms. In particular, in order to study the models by means of which the structure of a scientific theory is analyzed, representation theorems have to be stated, as they are the best insight into the structure of a complex theory (Suppes 2002, 51).

One of the key features envisaged by the process of representation is that of *invariance*. Intuitively, invariant is what is constant in

---

[17]See Chapter 2 for a comprehensive explanation of each of the four steps.

the representation of a structure, when the contextual features vary. In order to axiomatize a theory, it is necessary not only to define its set-theoretical models and to prove representation theorems about the theory, but also to individuate the fundamental properties that are invariant with respect to some important transformations. Such individuation is what for Suppes corresponds to seeking the objective meaning of a phenomenon, so that 'objective' can be identified with 'invariant with respect to a given framework of reference'.

4.2.2 A genuine empirical philosopher

On the basis of what was just said, we argue that set-theoretical axiomatization constitutes a unifying method in Suppes' philosophy. Different topics, such as the foundations of quantum mechanics and the study of language, are treated within the same formal framework, despite their macroscopic differences. At the same time, we deem that this does not constitute a unifying view forcing us to consider science as unitary and characterized by one and only one method. Suppes' pluralistic attitude is always present and works at two different levels: the first one, more evident, regards the diversity of topics under Suppes' attention, the second one concerns the impossibility of having a unifying view of science as Suppes has repeatedly stressed. Seeing a deep connection between the two is fairly obvious: it is only because Suppes has extensively worked in axiomatization of quantum mechan -ics, probability theory, in the analysis of language, and in psychology (just to mention the main areas of his interest), that he is able to give a very realistic picture of science. In this way science, far from being a monolith, characterized by permanent properties, is fragmented in specific fields, each with its peculiar methods and objects of analysis.

Accordingly, the detailed analysis of science plays a central role in Suppes' philosophical enterprise. Suppes defines himself in the following way: "I'm the only genuine empirical philosopher I know" (Suppes 1979b, 45). To investigate a scientific theory means to know how it *really* works in *real* scientific contexts. Only when this knowledge is acquired, is it possible to reconstruct the structure of the theory starting from its empirical base. This empirical[18] base, however, does not guarantee a straight way toward the theoretical reconstruction:

---

[18]We claim that empirical here is not used just in its common meaning of being related to experience, but in the stronger sense of keeping in mind all nuances of the experience itself.

this way may be tortuous and less direct than what expected by the idealized views proposed by many philosophers of science. Here Suppes' pragmatism plays a key role in giving back a realistic representation of science, together with the aim of a rational reconstruction of it.

This down-to-earth approach might seem to conflict with Suppes' advocacy of formal methods. However, it is possible to be formal, even while recognizing the importance of a pragmatic approach: data should be treated formally, when possible, *formal structures* can be mixed with *empirical structures*, and models representing theories can range from *models of data* to *models of theories*, giving rise to a full hierarchy of models, representing the different parts of a scientific enterprise. This does not mean that Suppes' account aims at constructing formally the whole science. This would be an obstacle to the commitment to the detailed analysis that Suppes does not want to give up. A formal (in Suppes' sense) treatment of science, when possible, is a useful guideline to reflect philosophically on the foundations of a science, but is not the whole story. It would be too naive for Suppes to think that a formal representation is able to exhaust the complexities of real science.

4.3 Historical and conceptual roots

Axiomatization, models, and set theory constitute the formal framework in which Suppes carries out his approach to the philosophy of science. Even before Suppes, formal methods were present in philosophy and, in particular, in philosophy of science. Think for example of the logical empiricism of the last century and its scientific conception of the world, with the logical reduction of philosophy to the analysis of language (see, for example, (Neurath 1973)). Moreover, formal methods are living today a revival in current formal epistemology (see, for instance, (Hendricks and Symons 2005)) aiming at formalizing different parts of philosophy. In this section we argue in favor of the origin of Suppes' concept of formalization in modern geometry and, even before that, in Aristotle's concept of sameness of form, as presented in the *De Anima*.

4.3.1 Formalization and the birth of modern geometry

Suppes' approach shows both commonalities and differences with the formal tradition of philosophy. What they share is the desire to fill the gap between philosophy and science; as Suppes states: "The use of such methods [formal methods] permits us to bring to the philosophy of science the standards of rigor and clarity that are an accepted part of the mathematical sciences" (Suppes 2002, 49). What is different in Suppes' work is a closer attention to axiomatization and to the axiomatic tradition.

The origin of the axiomatic method and its features are discussed in many of his writings (see, for example, (Suppes 2002) for a general presentation) where he acknowledges the roots of the axiomatic method in Greek geometry and mathematics. It would be too simplistic, however, to see just Euclid and Archimedes, in their attempts to achieve standards of rigor in theoretical and experimental science, as the roots of Suppes' methodology with its commitment to axiomatization.

According to Suppes (2002), quoting his mentor Ernest Nagel (1939), the modern conception of axiomatic method can be traced back to the birth of modern geometry in the 19th century and, in particular, to the work of the German mathematician Moritz Pasch (1843–1930). "Pasch was the one who saw very clearly this notion of formalism that consists of what is subjected to the isomorphic relation. The nature of formalization is relative to the properties that are going to be looked at in terms of isomorphic structure" (Interview, 14 December 2006). The main difference between ancient and modern axiomatization is a different degree of formalization (Suppes 1980a). In Euclid for example, considered the highest point in ancient mathematics, axiomatization is not fully carried out in formal terms. If Euclid's *Elements* constitute, from the one side, the basis for the birth of the axiomatic method, from the other side, they are not completely clear in separating formal issues from those concerning the application of geometry.

It is with Pasch in the 19th century, instead, that for the very first time the concept of *abstract axiom* is provided in clear terms. Abstract axioms are the axioms that do not have any intuitive content, but only the properties made explicit in the axioms themselves. This central result arises in the development of modern geometry that, starting from the beginning of the 19th century, rejects the traditional view of geometry as a quantitative science dealing with extension or space. Pasch, of course, is not the only player in the birth of modern geometry. J.V. Poncelet, J. D. Gergonne, H. G. Grassman and K. G. Von Staudt belong to the same tradition and, in different ways, take important steps in the direction of pure geometry.

The idea that geometry should employ abstract signs, such as the variables used in an algebra, has first been proposed by Jean-Victor Poncelet. The emphasis on abstract signs represents a radical transformation of geometry, even if this was not Poncelet's aim. It is only with Joseph Gergonne that the first formulation of the principle founding pure geometry is stated. This principle, called *principle of duality*, states that axioms are implicit definitions capable of having different concrete meanings associated with the variable-terms they contain (Nagel 1939, 224). This way, geometry is no more a science of magnitude, such as it used to be in the past, but becomes a *science of order*, that is to say:

> Pure geometry is a *formal* discipline operating with variables, which *may* but *need not* to be interpreted, and that pure geometry, in thus becoming abstract and without an intuitive content, is nevertheless an instrument for formulating identical structures in intuitively different subject matters. (Nagel 1939, 234)

Even if a new conception of geometry was implicit in the authors just mentioned, it is only with the writings of Pasch, however, that geometry is described as an *hypothetical-deductive system*. Axioms are implicit definitions of the terms they contain; hence geometry is formal in the sense that it is completely independent from intuition. Geometry is deductive and works independently from the meanings that can be associated to the concepts. Formalizing is the right answer in order to avoid the danger of intuitions in geometry, that would lead to discarding the deductive character of geometry. Nuclear propositions[19] expressed with common words should be replaced by arbitrary empty marks that could be filled differently in different occasions.
In Nagel's words:

> The result of such a formalization is an "empty frame" which expresses the structure of the set of nuclear propositions and which is alone relevant to the task of pure geometry. (Nagel 1939, 238)

So the development of geometry as a demonstrative science, in the sense of an hypothetico-deductive system, is due, among other things, to some of Pasch's ideas. His view on formalization is among the first of a series treating geometry as a system of logical relations between variables.

---

[19] According to Nagel (1939) nuclear propositions are those based on observations which have been indefinitely repeated, and which have been established so securely that mankind has forgotten their origin.

It is important to stress, however, that Pasch considered geometry as a natural science as well. Geometry is a natural science with regard to the origin of the axioms. On this issue Pasch was definitively an empiricist, as he claimed that the axioms of geometry are suggested by sensory intuitions, whose truth is established on the basis of sensory observations on bodies. It is worth noting that the appeal to intuition in this case should not be interpreted, as in the previous tradition: applied geometry is a natural science, but it is the natural science of *bodies*, and not of space or extension.

It is interesting at this point to identify some similarities between Pasch's mix of formalism and empiricism and Suppes' approach to the philosophy of science, where formalism (set-theoretical axiomatization of some parts of science) is accompanied with a pragmatic attitude and an attention to experience that soften the formal stances. The difference amongst the two approaches mainly concerns the level of integration between formalism and empiricism: in Pasch the two conceptions are related to different parts of mathematics, that is pure and applied mathematics, in Suppes there exists a real integration between the two in his general philosophical approach (see Chapter 5), and not just in mathematics. As for Suppes the whole philosophy of science needs to be more formal, the 'right' formalism needs to be adopted; and the right one is set-theoretical axiomatization. At the same time, Suppes believes that the attention to experience must not be forgotten, and a formal approach cannot be fully applied at the level of experience; nevertheless, formality can be very useful as a tool for abstracting important features from the messiness of the real world.

This mix of formalism and empiricism has not been followed in the tradition after Pasch. Mario Pieri, before, and David Hilbert, after, developed pure geometry in the direction of a pure formal approach. In their hands geometry becomes a *calculus*, whose axioms state the formal properties of the relations between points, lines, and planes. As a consequence, the relation between formal systems and experience is not clarified and the empirical import of Pasch's tradition has been completely forgotten. This is perhaps one of the reasons why formalism during the 20th century has been developed in this strong sense and foundational attitudes have spread over the whole of mathematics. Hilbert's influential *Grundlagen der Geometrie* (published for the first time in 1900) excludes any reference to intuition, and pure geometry is established as a calculus independent from its traditional association with space. In the modern axiomatic method the basic notions, on which the theory is going to be based, are not defined; they are considered, rather, as abstract entities, whose nature and concrete meaning do not really matter. What matters, instead, are the relations between these basic entities, as it is starting from these relations that axioms are defined. Hence, the properties deduced by such a formal theory are general and potentially applicable to different objects.

Even with minor differences, it is the tradition starting from Pasch and coming to a complete formalization with Hilbert that constitutes Suppes' background in formalizing. The history of geometry in the 19th century moves toward an increasing abstractness of language and the formalization of its procedures. Knowledge is not identified with its object anymore, but it is a sort of manipulation of symbols. As Nagel points out:

> The concepts of structure, isomorphism, and invariance, which have been fashioned out of the materials to which the principle of duality is relevant, dominate research in mathematics, logic, and the sciences of nature. (Nagel 1939, 254)

It is worth noting that structure, isomorphism and invariance are also the central concepts of Suppes' axiomatization and constitute the pillars of his approach.

4.3.2   Aristotle's sameness of form

The relation between structure, isomorphism, and invariance is expressed by the concept of *structural isomorphism*. This is the property representing the fact that two objects have the same form, not in absolute terms, but according to their structure. Two models of a scientific theory, for example, are isomorphic if they are structurally identical, while finer-grained differences that may arise from their definitions are ignored. This way, the invariant features of a scientific theory are displayed. The concept of structural isomorphism has emerged with its current meaning, as seen in the last subsection, during the development of modern geometry: it is the formal, structural version of the concept of *sameness of form* (see Chapter 2).

However, even before the advent of modern geometry, the concept of sameness of form plays an important role in the process of knowledge and in the representation lying behind it. In particular,

Pasch's structural isomorphism and Aristotle's conception of sameness of form share a great deal, as Suppes has recently stressed (Interview, 7 December 2006). Aristotle's conception of sameness of form is mainly described in the *De Anima*, which also contains his doctrine of *form* and *matter*. According to Suppes, these ideas represent one of the conceptual roots of modern formalization. The process from perception to abstraction, as described by Aristotle in the *De Anima*, resembles the key steps of the process of formalizing that ends up in the modern concept of structural isomorphism. If Suppes' interest in Aristotle's thought is already well known, here we argue in favor of some similarities between the way he intends the concept of structural isomorphism and Aristotle's doctrine of forms.

Aristotle's theory of perception is mainly described in the *De Anima*, where he investigates psychological phenomena and, in particular, the nature of soul and body. According to Aristotle, *perception* is the first step in the process of knowledge. However, perception is not sufficient as it lacks the systematicity required for knowledge; therefore, a series of further steps needs to be performed in order to acquire complete knowledge.

According to the doctrine described in the *De Anima*, this process of abstraction starts from the activity of recognizing similarities. Sameness of form seems to be the most intuitive and immediate concept to build up knowledge. If we want to know *if* two triangles are congruent[20] we need first to check if the sides and the angles are congruent. But *how* do we know that triangles are congruent, namely that they have the *same form*? We know that by subdividing the problem in its parts, by decomposing it in its three sides and three angles. This subdivision is the first step to move from pure perception to abstraction: the sameness of form cannot be detected perceptually, but it is the result of a process of decomposition in order to find the important features of an object.

In Aristotle, the view of body and soul is strongly connected to the doctrine of form and matter. More precisely, what is presented in the *De Anima* is an instance of Aristotle's *hylomorphism*, a conceptual framework underlying many Aristotelian works (Shields 2005). The soul is the *form* of the body, which is the *matter* of the soul. The notions

---

[20]We owe this suggestion to Patrick Suppes who expressed it in an interview of December 2006.

of form and matter are developed in the context of a general theory of causation where the form is the actuality of the body which is its matter. A matter is something *potentially*, until it acquires an actualizing form and so becomes *actually* something.

Nutrition, perception, and mind are the soul's faculties: nutrition is the broadest one and is possessed by all living organisms; perception is possessed by animals and humans; mind is possessed only by humans. For our purpose, perception and mind are the most interesting, as they concern *discrimination* (the former) and *abstraction* (the latter) involved in the process of knowledge.

In Aristotle's terms, perception is an *alteration* taking place between two different agents: the object able of acting and the capacity able to be affected. The affected thing receives the form of the affecting agent and 'becomes like' the agent. This alteration is a sort of *informing*, as change is explained by the acquisition of a form by something that is capable of receiving it. Perception affects only the entities capable of perceiving the perceptible forms of the objects. In other words, a subject is able to perceive an object if this subject has the capacity of receiving the object's *sensible form*. Moreover, the object must be able to act upon that capacity and to inform it. The result is that the relevant capacity of the subject becomes identical with that form:

> The sensitive faculty is potentially such as the sensible object is in actuality. While it is being acted upon, it is not yet similar, but, when once it has been acted upon, it is assimilated and has the same character as the sensible object. (Aristotle 1907), *De Anima*, 418a6–418a10

Mind is, in a sense, analogous to perception; as perception involves the reception of a form by the appropriate faculty, thinking involves the reception of an *intelligible form* by the appropriate *intellectual faculty*. Also in this case, a subject is able to think an object if this subject has the capacity of receiving the object's intelligible form. The object must be able to act upon that capacity and to inform it. The result is that the relevant capacity of the subject becomes identical with that form. Here we have a very peculiar view of thought consisting in the process of a mind acquiring the *same form* of the object by which it has been affected. The mind, of course, must be prepared; that means it needs to have the capacity of receiving the intelligible form of the object being known.

> The soul is all existent things. For they are all either objects of sensa-

tion or objects of thought; and knowledge and sensation are in a manner identical with their respective objects. [...] It follows that the faculties must be identical, if not with the things themselves, then with their forms. The things themselves they are not, for it is not the stone which is in the soul, but the form of the stone. (Aristotle 1907) *De Anima*, 431b20–432a2

As already seen, the Aristotelian conception of thinking is strongly based on the concept of sameness of form. The mind and the object affected by thought must have the same form. In other words, to think is analogous to be informed by the object that is thought. As a result, the mind acquires the same form of the object it is thinking. To do that, the mind needs to have the (at least potential) capacity to receive that form.

The concept of sameness of form, of course, can be intended in different ways. The most reasonable idea is that perception and thought involve acquiring the structural features of the object of perception and thought. A modern way to express this is that, in perception and thought, the relevant capacities of the subject become identical with the form to be perceived or thought and this is to say that these faculties of the soul are isomorphic with the forms of the objects perceived or thought. Structural isomorphism is a more precise way to express the concept of sameness of form and, in a sense, can be intended as a stronger notion than Aristotle's sameness of form.

> The relevant point here is that the notion of sameness of form corresponds very closely to the concept of isomorphism that I have been arguing for as a central concept of representation: the concept of form catches nicely that of isomorphism in the sense that the form does not thereby refer to all the properties of the candle, but only to the properties perceived by the various senses of sight, touch, etc. This kind of restriction to the properties considered is, as already noted in earlier discussions, characteristic of any workable notion of isomorphism. (Suppes 2002, 82)

And, together with the concept of sameness of form, Tarski's ideas about formalism constitute the background of Suppes' theorizing about formal methods and isomorphism.

> [...] So there's a kind of background all the way from Aristotle to the 19th century. My own idea about formalization comes from that background, the background that formed in the first half of the 20th century [...] and I guess that in my own case the work of Tarski, which was

so absolutely clear, really was a big influence in my own getting really clear about formalization. Tarski is one of the wonderful examples of having extraordinary clarity about formalism. There are other people, but in terms of me, personally, it was Tarski, whom I met when I was very young. When I started teaching at Stanford in 1950, I used to go to his seminars. (Interview, 14 December 2006)

This very idea is clearly expressed in one of our latest conversations with Suppes, in which he explains his program in the philosophy of brain, acknowledging its theoretical roots in Aristotle as well.

Now, I actually have this proto-article I would like to write, called "The Brain's Anomalies" in the sense that we are not going to find something localized and say, "Oh, there's abstract meaning." It won't be like that. It's going to be something more like the isomorphisms that are surely there in much of perception, as Aristotle proposed in *De Anima*. Such an isomorphism, however, is not between mental objects as such. It is between one kind of matter and another kind of matter. So out there is a scene we perceive and inside the brain is another little glob of matter that isomorphically represents features of the perceived scene. Not the whole thing, but parts of it. So really the way the brain works is by isomorphism between processes in the brain and processes outside. One might say that is a reductive thesis, and of course it is. But the nature of these isomorphisms is cognitive. That is how the cognitive machinery is operating, it is by using isomorphism. I am talking now about perception, but it applies to representations of language, which we can think of perceptually. Now, you see, of course, the early Greek thinkers did not put as much emphasis on process, but in many senses Aristotle's theory of sensible forms in perception in the *De Anima* is very much in the spirit of how I am commenting. So, as I like to point out, when we talk about perception, the thesis about the isomorphism is very much like Aristotle's concept of form. The morphism part comes from the Greek word meaning "form". The analysis of Aristotle is a little short on the whole process, but that is not surprising. The basic idea is that what the mind is grasping, when you put it in those old-fashioned terms, is the form, and that fits well in talk about isomorphism between the outside processes and those inside the brain. So that is a first step, in important essentials due to Aristotle and his predecessors. Later the excellent commentaries of Aquinas and others over a long period, including Themistius' well known paraphrase, written in the late Hellenistic period and read during the early Renaissance, as the main treatise on psychology, are of permanent value, better guides in many ways to the fundamental processes than a lot of thinking that goes on in contemporary cognition. The opinions I am expressing here are controversial, but they need saying. (Interview, 31 March 2009)

4.4 The sense of formalizing

The process of formalization that informs Suppes' approach to the philosophy of science is characterized by an axiomatic stance. The tight connection between axiomatizing and formalizing may create the illusion that the two processes coincide. In order to avoid any misunderstanding, we deem it important to clarify in this section these two terms and their relationship. After having explained the general sense of Suppes' formalization, we discuss his motivations for a formal approach to the philosophy of science.

4.4.1 Axiomatization and formalization

Axiomatization is a process starting from the determination of a finite number of principles describing the fundamental concepts of a body of knowledge. In other words, it is a method for organizing the concepts and the statements of a given discipline. From the primitive concepts of a discipline, other concepts can be derived, and axiomatization takes care of the transition from axioms to theorems through the use of rules of inference. Even if, generally speaking, it is possible to say that axiomatization is the starting point and necessary condition for formalizing (Novaes 2006), it should be noted that different degrees of formality in axiomatizing may exist. Euclid, for example, widely considered as the father of the axiomatic method, provides an axiomatization of geometry carried out without the use of any formal language. In Euclid's *Elements*, formality deals with the activity of structuring knowledge starting from its primitive elements, and not with the use of a formal language.

The concept of formal can be intended in a number of ways.[21] As already seen, Euclid's way is not exactly in the sense of modern axiomatization in which, under the influence of Pasch, Peano, Hilbert and many others, the concept of formal is considered as an abstraction from the content in the direction of a pure 'form'.

In a very general sense, this meaning of formalization is related to the use of a formal language for representing knowledge about phe-

---

[21]See Novaes (2006) for a review of the different ways in which the concept of formal can be intended and MacFarlane (2000) for a discussion on the ways formality can be adopted in logic.

nomena. This can be reflected in the use of formulas typical of many branches of science: their purpose is to express knowledge about the world in a quantitative and, at the same time, synthetic way.

In the standard mathematical framework adopted by Suppes, formalization is deeply related to axiomatization. More precisely, for Suppes to axiomatize means to give set-theoretical definitions with the axioms representing the primitive principles of a theory or, more generally, of a body of knowledge. Thus, formalizing is connected to the concept of structural isomorphism and, hence, to a way of looking at the fundamental properties of a theory in terms of isomorphic structures.

It is possible, however, to have a more precise and restricted definition of formal, where formal involves the use of a completely formal language, such as first-order logic. Accordingly, formalization is the process by which a logical or mathematical field takes one of the following forms: a class of *signs*, a class of *well-defined formulas*, a class of *axioms*, a class of *rules of inference*, and a class of *proofs* (Politis 1965). In other words, full formalization means to have a formally specified language that, recursively, defines all the well-formed formulas from a fixed vocabulary. In this case the relation to axiomatization is given by the fact that this formal language is used to state axioms.

To sum up, it is possible to distinguish three main conceptions of formal. The first one is the most general, where formal is related to the use of formulas and symbols to represent knowledge, namely formalization in the sense of standard mathematics. The second one is more connected to axiomatization and means related to the form and abstracted from the matter. The third one is the most technical, where formal refers to the use of a language which is completely specified from a formal standpoint to state the axioms of a theory and all the well-formed formulas are defined recursively.

The second and the third conceptions are mutually strongly connected both from a historical and a conceptual point of view. According for example to Politis (1965, 365) "Contemporary developments in both logic and mathematics have refined the axiomatic presentation reaching the level of formalization", intended in the third sense stated above. Moreover, once directed toward formalization (always in the third sense), parts of traditional philosophy, such as logic, have developed into autonomous and scientific disciplines (Suppes 1954).

Logic, in particular, has been seen as an inspiration in the development of the scientifically-oriented philosophy typical of the logical empiricism. Logical formalization is surely the type of formal method that has received more attention from philosophers in the last century (Suppes 1979a). On the other hand, Suppes has stressed in many publications the limits of such formalization, which is not able to express the complexity of most scientific theories. Any formal language defined in this way is an idealization from the concrete languages used in science. If a certain degree of abstraction from the messiness of experience is necessary in the process of knowledge, at the same time it is important to avoid the illusion that experience can be fully captured by a formal language, even by a very expressive one.

It is mainly for this reason that Suppes intends the activity of formalizing in the philosophy of science in the second broadest sense. Formalization is an adequate representation of scientific theories, obtained by letting emerge their invariant structures. At the center of his formal approach lies the process of axiomatization, but not the adoption of a language which is formally fully specified.

> Luckily we can pursue a program of axiomatization without constructing any formal languages. The viewpoint I am advocating is that the basic methods appropriate for axiomatic studies in the empirical sciences are not metamathematical (and thus syntactical and semantical), but set-theoretical. To axiomatize the theory of a particular branch of empirical science in the sense I am advocating is to give a definition of a set-theoretical notion. (Suppes 1954, 244)

As it is clear in the above quotation, the Suppesian idea of formalization is a process of axiomatization giving the form of a theory, while abstracting from finer-grade differences. He never forgets, however, that matter, as well, is always present and that trying to eliminate it would result in a completely unrealistic picture of reality and, consequently, of science. This is the reason why formalization cannot be the only method of philosophical analysis and it is subjected to numerous limitations. Before considering the context of applicability of Suppes' conception of formalization and its limits, we need to analyze with more details what are the motivations behind the process of formalization in Suppes' thought.

4.4.2   Formalization: reasoning as a computation

In asking why Suppes aims at introducing such a formal approach in the philosophy of science, we should not forget that his main challenge for formalizing is to add rigor to the philosophy of science, while preserving its richness and its ability to reflect all the details of science. In (Suppes 1954), a paper that can be considered as the opening of his philosophical program, he states the sense of his formalization in philosophy: "My first general programmatic proposal is that philosophers of science set themselves the task of axiomatizing the theory of all developed branches of empirical sciences" (Suppes 1954, 244). And again some years later, he further clarifies: "In the context of such clarification and construction, a primary method of philosophical analysis is that of formalizing and axiomatizing the concepts and theories of fundamental importance in a given domain of science" (Suppes 1968, 653).

The general motivation behind formalizing lies in the rigor and clarity promoted by a formal approach. One of the possible ways to achieve accuracy and precision is in the formal approach advocated by Suppes. Its main feature is to be a method for representing the primitive notions of a body of knowledge in a rigorous and unambiguous way. At the same time, it is not characterized by the use of a completely formal language and, therefore, it does not suffer the limitations of it.

From a historical point of view, any form of formalization can be seen as a way to introduce methods of computation in reasoning. According to this view, knowledge needs to be *externalized*, that is to say that the path that has been followed for a certain reasoning should be made explicit, in order to guarantee a better degree of control and, thus, of correctness. For instance, when one is making a complex calculation (think, for example, the multiplication of two of large numbers), it is certainly easier to use paper and pencil instead of doing mental calculations. With externalization, one is better guaranteed not only about the correctness of the final result but also about the process adopted in achieving this final result: he or she has a way of checking the correctness of the whole process, step by step. If the primary reason for the process of externalization lies in the desire of accuracy, there is also a skeptical attitude not to be underestimated. The latter has to do with a form of skepticism about honesty. If you do not completely trust somebody, you want some kind of record of things, namely ways of keeping track of processes and results.

> Formalization is like introducing methods of computation in general reasoning. And what is important about methods of computation is that everybody recognizes you couldn't carry around in your head really accurate arithmetic of all kinds, you are going to make a lot of mistakes [...]. What is important about calculation needed to be externalized. Part of the reason wasn't just because of accuracy, but it was also because of skepticism about honesty: you want some records of things [...] So one of the virtues of formalization is making thinking, deduction and reasoning more similar to calculation. The formalization consists of having very exact external representations. (Interview, 5 December 2006)

Externalization can be intended in a more specific way as well. In this case it is called *explicitness* (Suppes 1968) and is the property of making the meaning of a set of concepts clear, in order to understand the most elementary properties characterizing a theory. In setting the axioms representing the core of a scientific theory, the elementary properties of that theory are made manifest. The example given by (Suppes 1968) is the set of axioms stated by Kolmogorov for the probability theory. They represent an explicit analysis of the formal structure of probability, whose meaning, thanks to externalization, is carried out in an explicit fashion. On the one hand, this formalization has served to state what the elementary properties of probability are. On the other hand, it promoted the discussion about the philosophical and conceptual analysis of probability.

Accordingly, another virtue of formalization deals with a sort of *idealization*. A formal representation is always the outcome of a simplification for the sake of clarity: by isolating important aspects, it contributes to bringing them to light. This applies, for example, to formal models of rational behavior and rational belief in which the complexities of real life are left out and the standards of rationality are higher than those of real agents (Hansson 2000).

Another motivation for formalizing is *generality*. Generality deals with the representation of just the essential properties of a scientific theory, leaving aside inessential features. To leave aside the inessential features of a scientific theory permits us to focus just on its core parts, providing a means for seeing the forest in spite of the trees. According to generality, it is possible to establish what the *minimal assumptions* to express a theory are and how this theory can be formulated in terms of these minimal assumptions. This is a way to test our understanding of a theory: if we are able to answer the question "What are the minimal assumptions in terms of which a theory can be formulated?", then we can provide an accurate analysis of the foundations of that theory. To ask what is a minimal but sufficient set of assumptions for psychoanalysis, for example, represents a serious problem (Suppes 1968).

The clarification of the conceptual problems carried out by methods of formalization can be observed also in the process of *standardization*. Standardization is one of the most desirable consequences of formalization, in regards to both terminology and methods. This really matters in those branches of sciences where even the most basic concepts are controversial, and we can say that it permits us to achieve at least a certain level of objectivity. Moreover, standardization makes communication easier across scientific disciplines and allows comparisons and exchanges between them.

It is important not to forget, however, the computational purpose of formalization just mentioned. Formalization aims at introducing methods of computation in general reasoning, making reasoning more similar to calculation. If we consider an axiomatic system, we can define calculation as the path to construct proofs starting from the axioms and using the rules of inference, more generally the path to infer new knowledge from previous knowledge using just axioms and inference rules.

To summarize, we can see the general motivations for formalization, and the role of philosophy of science in formalizing, in Suppes' words:

> The role of philosophy in science is to clarify conceptual problems and to make explicit the foundational assumptions of each scientific discipline. The clarification of conceptual problems or the building of an explicit logical foundation are tasks that are neither intensely empirical nor mathematical in character. They may be regarded as proper philosophical tasks directly relevant to science. (Suppes 1968, 653)

Suppes, however, is aware of the limits of formalization and claims that:

> To argue that such formalization is one important method of clarification is not in any sense to claim that it is the only method of philosophical analysis [...] Formalization will not answer all questions nor solve all problems. (Suppes 1968, 653)

Besides the general advantages of formalization presented above, it seems important to discuss the actual applicability of formalization intended as axiomatization in set-theoretical terms. This is the next topic. It will turn out that formalizing philosophy of science and using formal philosophy do have limits. Now it is time to clearly point out what these limits are.

4.5 The context for formalization

The term *formal* may have various meanings and in this chapter we have tried to clarify the sense Suppes ascribes to it. This chapter would not be complete, however, without considering the context of applicability of the formal approach just described. By discussing the applicability of this formal method, its limits will be clarified as well.

4.5.1 Applicability

As already pointed out, Suppes does not aim at applying formal methods to the whole philosophy of science, but he focuses on the foundations of science which are the context of applicability of set-theoretical formalization (see for example Suppes (2002, Ch. 2)). In thinking about foundations, Suppes believes that set-theoretical formalization is the correct framework for a proper philosophical analysis of the concepts that form and characterize a scientific theory. He is fully aware that the context of the foundations of a science is different from its practice. In the latter case, more detailed models are needed, not just for representation, but also for empirical predictions. Working physicists, for example, have neither the time nor will to formalize in the set-theoretical style.

Physicists, in particular, even blame the process of formalization (*qua* axiomatization) as too restrictive. This is because, on the theoretical side, it is almost impossible to reduce the complexity of various parts of physics to an axiomatized system. Furthermore, on the practical side, they do not have time for such a complex task, especially when it is not useful to achieve concrete results.

Physicists of course use formalization in a general sense: this is precisely the first meaning of formal described in Section 4.4. They adopt the minimal degree of formality which is that involved in the use of symbols and formulas. The latter are required to apply and exploit computational methods that are an essential part of physics today and, without exaggerating, of most empirical sciences. Most solutions cannot be calculated by hand, so computational methods and computers running them are undoubtedly required. Nevertheless, to achieve a good capability of computation, formalization in the Suppes' sense is not required. It is evident that the majority of scientific papers are not written in set-theoretical style. Science nowadays is often a matter of rushing to get there first and scientists do not have time for such 'delicacies' as axiomatization.

What are then the advantages for science in engaging in a long process, such as formalization intended in the axiomatic connotation? As said in Section 4.4.2, there are a number of motivations in engaging in formalization. These reasons primarily deal with *idealization*, for the sake of simplicity, and *explicitness*, namely with an elucidation of the core properties. So we claim that formalizing is the type of analysis that is usually carried out by philosophy. The fact that formalizing is mainly a philosophical task is probably the reason why this style of formalization is not common in science, even if there are exceptions such as, for instance, pure mathematics and some parts of economics.

At the same time, it is undeniable that the practice of formalizing in the general sense is typical of science. The difference between science and philosophy of science with regard to formalization concerns not only the different type of formal approach (the former related to the use of symbols and formulas, the latter to the construction of axiomatic systems), but the different purpose behind it. The kind of formal approach carried out by science aims at allowing the effective computations required in many fields of empirical science. The formal approach carried out in the philosophy of science (and in particular the set-theoretical axiomatization proposed by Suppes), instead, has its primary goal in a rigorous and clear analysis of different parts of science and, in particular, in the study of the foundations of scientific disciplines.

At first sight this distinction between philosophy of science and science may appear unjustified, according in particular to the following words:

> [...] a distinction between philosophy of science and science is in itself incorrect. In many ways I am sympathetic with such a summary of Quine's view, namely, that philosophy should be mainly philosophy of

science and philosophy of science should mainly itself be science. This is a way of saying that philosophy is not privy to any special methods different from the methods used in the sciences. (Suppes 2006, 32)

This position is in line with Suppes' self-identification as a philosopher of science, but also as an empirical scientist, as philosophy of science is mainly science and adopts scientific methods. However, in the same passage, he recognizes that:

I certainly very much agree with these ideas [Quine's view on science and philosophy of science], but also think that there are special aspects of problems that are of particular philosophical interest and often cultivated only by philosophers (Suppes 2006, 32).

The kinds of genuine philosophical problems are, for example, those faced by current philosophers of physics that, instead of developing abstract theories of space and time with no connection to current physics, make 'philosophical commentaries' on the results achieved by working physicists. For Suppes those philosophical commentaries can enjoy a formal treatment such as the set-theoretical axiomatization just described.

Here the effort put in developing the formal framework required for the analysis is rewarded by a better clarity, an augmented rigor, more precision, and a complete accuracy. Unfortunately, the kind of 'scientific philosophy' advocated is not very often applied in philosophy. Particularly disappointing for Suppes is the case of the philosophy of mind that, instead of considering the latest scientific results of neuroscience and psychology, is still connected to the old philosophical tradition. It is only by starting from a detailed analysis of a scientific discipline, by concretely knowing its way of working and its latest results, that it is possible for Suppes to practice the philosophy of science.

The connection between axiomatization and philosophical analysis which is at the core of Suppes' work may induce us to believe that formalizing concerns just the theoretical part of science, like pure mathematics. Instead, the representation of science and the consequent philosophical analysis carried out in the set-theoretical framework pertain to empirical sciences as well (see Chapter 5). Even the empirical level (that is usually the most difficult to deal with, due to its richness) deserves a formal treatment. Suppes' famous models of data and hierarchy of models prove that it is possible to adopt a rigorous approach, even in the face of experience. Models of data are an abstraction from experience; the abstraction that allows us to formally treat parts of the experience itself.

4.5.2 Limits

It would be a mistake, however, to believe that the whole scientific activity, made up of procedures, practices, and behaviors (besides all theoretical knowledge involved) could be formalized and transformed in an axiomatic system. It would be an unjustified oversimplification to look at science as resting upon solid and sharp foundations.

For these reasons, we deem particularly important to stress the limitations of applicability of Suppes' formal approach, as in some cases these limitations have not been considered. It is a quite widespread misunderstanding to view Suppes as the proposer of a complete application of the formal approach to the philosophy of science. Thus, it is worth claiming that formalization in set-theoretical style does not work as a demarcation between 'good' and 'bad' philosophy, but it is just a valuable way to represent scientific theories and to let emerge invariant structures in science.

Neither we can trace this demarcation limit based on the axiomatizability or non axiomatizability of a scientific theory:

> We have to be careful! Because after all, there are well known theories about elementary mathematics that are not axiomatizable. Well, first, what do we mean by *axiomatizable*? First we can mean in the strict sense, that we can have a finite set of axioms; secondly, we can mean that we can have a recursive set of axioms and usually recursivity is required for the axioms. So, you do want axioms for which you have a decision procedure for deciding whether or not a given formula is an axiom or not. You don't want to have a problem with no decision procedure as to whether a given statement is an axiom, that would be slightly bizarre. Then, of course, you can have the business of axiomatizing from outside, in terms of an exterior characterization or extrinsic characterization, but you can't give, with limited means, for example, an intrinsic characterization. A typical example is you can't axiomatize measurement or physics starting from scratch from first-order logic and have a numerical representation, because you cannot axiomatize the Archimedean axiom or its equivalent, in first-order logic. So, I think axiomatizability doesn't mark the difference between science and non science or mathematics and non mathematics, I think it marks the difference between a subject that, within a given domain or set of methods,

can be given a very clear characterization and one that can't. (Interview, 20 November 2003)

Formalizing presents several risks.[22] First of all, formal models tend to be oversimplified. This is particularly risky in Suppes' case as he promotes a detailed philosophical analysis of science. So, while reducing the primitive notions of a theory to a very minimum, close attention has to be paid to choose the right form of simplification that does not neglect aspects of the world that have instead to be considered.

Moreover, formalization is often committed to an enigmatic style: choices in formalizing are carried out without explanation and often remain implicit. The danger in this case is to alienate formal methods from philosophers and scholars not used to them. Sometimes, an explicit explanation of the reasons for some choices is the best way to clarify the formal framework, while completing it with informal methods as well.

But how far is it possible to apply formal methods? Are formal methods the only available tool for the philosophy of science? These two questions are strongly connected and the answer to the first one partially suggests the answer for the second. It is important to stress that a sharp boundary between formal and informal methods does not exist. We may say in general that formal methods are more easily applied when the field is very precise and well delimited. At the same time, however, Suppes suggests a formal treatment also of parts of experience and of empirical data (see Chapter 5). Hence, a mix of formal and informal methods is required: it would be an extreme oversimplification to think that, even in pure mathematics (to consider the most formal case), a set-theoretical axiomatization could exhaust the philosophical analysis of the matter.

If we look, in particular, at experience, its formalization is not easily attainable: the world is not simple and to believe in its complete formalization is a quite ingenuous attitude. This does not mean philosophers of science must give up formalizing. Rather, it means that they need to be aware that every process of abstraction, even if it is a natural attitude in knowledge, always leaves something besides.

To do scientific work with the data you must abstract from this rich experience, this full experience [...] and you have procedures and instruments, and you know the instruments the way you know other per-

---

[22]See Hansson (2000) for a detailed examination of the dangers of formalization.

sons: you know a lot about them but you seldom know everything [...]
so you can't write down a formalization of how an instrument does
behave [...] But you get something from those data. Those data themselves often can be in a complicated form. You abstract from them and
that's the way you reach models of data. (Interview, 14 December 2006)

Here, we can observe the lesson Suppes learned from the pragmatist tradition. By starting from the detailed observation of scientific experience, it is natural to discover that believing in a sharp and definite
foundation of science is a mistake: "formalizing the world is a mistaken project" (Interview, 14 December 2006). The emphasis on practice shows that evidence is not the same for everybody and perception
is fallible. Knowledge is nevertheless still possible: the limits of knowledge do not prevent knowledge itself and it is certainly possible to
know also what cannot be formalized (Interview, 9 August 2002).

It's simply a mistake, a philosophical mistake, to think that there are
such sharp foundations. To search for such foundations is a mistake. I
regard as one of the major philosophical ideas of pragmatism in philosophy to get people to shake up their habit of mind, to change their habit
of thinking. [...] Problems have rational solutions in the sense of deduc-
tion from some set of meaningful, agreed upon, substantive principles:
it doesn't work like that. [...] The application of theory in science to experimentation, to empirical data, has conflicting norms, and if you don't
understand about these conflicting norms, it just means that you're still
innocent about the facts of life. (Interview, 9 December 2006)

The case of foundations of mathematics carried out starting from
the beginning of the last century is for Suppes revealing of this conflicting attitude. From the one side, a group of philosophers, logicians,
and open-minded mathematicians demanded the search for a single
and strong foundation of mathematics. From the other side, working
mathematicians did not feel the same need and rarely had a detailed
view on the problems connected to the foundations of mathematics.
After some years, the first group discovered the impossibility of a
strong foundation for mathematics. The foundational program went
into a crisis, but the attitude for the search of foundations, even if
weakened, did not stop.

Nonetheless, even in the study of the foundations of mathematics,
where the use of formal methods is prominent, Suppes finds some
exceptions:

There are philosophically and foundationally important points of mathematics that are interesting to philosophy of science and the foundations of mathematics, but particularly philosophy of science—so for example, the history of the theory of constructions in geometry, which also has applications for architects. You normally formulate this in a non set- theoretical way. It's very standard to do that. You can formulate it in first-order language if you want to be formal, but they're often given rather informally, and you often concentrate on the student learning how to make the constructions, or to do the constructions, whichever language you prefer. And that's a matter of considerable conceptual interest for the long history. I remind you that the Greeks very clearly distinguished this. *Teorema*—theorems, we would call them—were one thing, *problema*, which were constructions, were something quite different. Constructions were ended by saying, "and this was what was to be done," and in the case of theorems, "this was what was to be demonstrated or proved," depending how you translate the Greek. This distinction is a little bit lost in much modern teaching in mathematics, but was very clear to the Greeks. To show its importance, Proposition 1 of Book 1 of Euclid is a *problema*: "How to bisect a line segment." It's not the proof of a theorem. So that distinction ranges a long ways, and where it is really powerful over on the doing side, ordinarily set-theoretical methods are not used very much. (Interview, 1 April 2009)

But there is still another important point to make: the incapability of formal methods to deal with some part of science has a direct consequence, i.e. that such a method (as well as all other methods, in Suppes' opinion) cannot play the role of overarching means for the unification of the sciences.

The fantasy of explicit formality, with elimination of all need for intuitive judgment, is recognized as an outmode concept, even in mathematics. Hilbert's program of formalism was upset years ago by Gödel's incompleteness theorems and the gap between formal theories of proof, for example, and actual mathematical practice, requiring judgments of all kinds, is now widely acknowledged. (Suppes 1984, 216)

The philosophical push for foundations can be found again today in Suppes' approach toward science and his way of turning philosophy of science into a well balanced mix of formal and informal methods. His pluralism and pragmatism prevent him from believing in the old dream of the unique foundation. Suppes is aware that, if some foundations are to be found (not certainly for the whole of science, but in specific scientific disciplines), "they are going to be shaky but, still, can be useful" (Interview, 9 December 2006).

There is somewhere a beautiful quotation from de Finetti in which as part of defending the Bayesian use of far-from-certain prior information in making decisions, he says that it is better to build on sand than on a void. I believe we can rephrase this remark and say something that is important for philosophy. When it comes to matters of knowledge, real houses are always built on sand and never on rock. (Suppes 1974b, 283)

5

Probabilistic Thinking and Experimental Practices

This chapter presents another important aspect of originality in Suppes' philosophy of science, namely a new way of treating empirical practices through the use of formal methods and the application of an approach based on formal models of experiments.

First of all, Suppes claims it is important for philosophers to study in a rigorous way experimental procedures, but he encourages a more comprehensive attitude than the one traditionally put forward. The study of experimentation includes many different facets, that must all be studied thoroughly if one wants to build a serious theory, starting from a theory of instrumentation, where the knowledge contained in manuals has to be explicitly taken into consideration, to the study of apprenticeship and training of the experimenters.

Another very important issue, which is central with respect to a theory of experimentation, is of course that concerning how to treat errors. According to Suppes, it is important to realize that mature disciplines cannot consider errors as accidents anymore; they have rather to become a direct subject of study, given the fact that contemporary science does not see them only as result of mistaken behavior of the experimenter, but are intrinsically part of the subject matter of science. This is because contemporary science shows a novel picture of nature, a picture in which determinism is no more tenable.

The indeterministic character that Suppes detects in nature can be more adequately dealt with by using probabilistic means and this fact is surely acknowledged by Suppes and strongly informs his approach, which he himself calls probabilistic empiricism, a locution that expresses both its conviction about the centrality of experimental practices in science and the interest in using a probabilistic apparatus within such practices.

Finally, we will try to briefly show how this shift towards an indeterministic view about reality gives as a consequence a new way to conceptualize causation, which can no more be seen as a clear explanation of the link between rigidly connected events, but must rather become a kind of theoretic instrument that enables us to infer the occurrence of future events on the basis of the observation of past events.

A final remark about this chapter is in order and is relative to a difference that it bears with all other chapters in the way in which it is structured. While other chapters can be mainly interpreted as commentaries about the various aspects of Suppes' philosophy, this last chapter mostly revolves around a couple of recent interviews. So, while in other chapters we talk about Suppes, in this one in a sense we talk with him. The reason for this choice is given by the fact that most of the material contained in these interviews has not been formalized in articles yet, so it is novel and unpublished and we believe that the best way to render the complexity and the recent evolution of Suppes' thought is to listen to him while he freely talks about it.

5.1 Experiments and experimental procedures

In this section we will present Suppes' approach with respect to his analysis of the connections between the theoretical and the experimental sides of scientific disciplines and, in particular, of the continuous and bidirectional interplay between theories and experimental data. We will start from his interest in theories of experimentation.

5.1.1 The importance of apprenticeship

A possible starting point for the analysis of such an interplay is from the limitations on the application of Suppes' favorite method: the representation in set-theoretical models.

> In science, you only need to open nearly any scientific journal to recognize the limitations. It's not standard practice to write science using a mathematical framework that is explicitly stated in a set-theoretical fashion. There are exceptions to this, in mathematical physics, corresponding parts of chemistry, computational biology, in economics (particularly in mathematical economics), and standard physics. But if you open the pages of *Physics Review Letters* (PRL), where more new physics

is published than anyplace else in the world, you can read a thousand pages and not see any really explicit use of careful set-theoretical language. That is because physicists use mathematics in an easy and informal way, just as they don't use theorems—you can also read a thousand pages and not find a single theorem stated. (Interview, 1 April 2009)

Suppes recognizes that the use of set theory is not common practice in many branches of science and he also quotes an example taken from his own personal experience.

And I'll tell you a wonderful anecdote about that. I've only really published, together with my co-author Acacio de Barros, one paper in *Physics Review Letters*; it was about quantum entanglement for triples of particles, what are called GHZ-type experiments, for Greenberger, Horne, and Zeilinger. For these GHZ experiments we derived inequalities corresponding to the Bell inequalities for the Bell-type experiments, for four particles with four different measurements. We put the results in a theorem, but the editor who accepted the article said, "We accept the article, but would you please remove the theorems? Physicists don't like to read theorems; give the results, but put them in informal language." We did remove the theorems, and we just put something in informally—"We can show the following results," or something like that—in the text. The argument remained the same, of course. (Interview, 1 April 2009)

There is indeed a place where set-theoretical methods are first class citizens, namely foundational studies of all scientific disciplines. But, interestingly enough, Suppes shows that even when talking about foundations, there is something that escapes the treatment in set-theoretical terms, as we can read in this long quotation.

Now, there is still another place where it has little applicability even to foundations. I'll mention this and one other case, but this case is perhaps the most important, and that, as I've mentioned already in these conversations, is emphasizing practice in the context of experimentation. The way to becoming a competent experimenter is usually by being an apprentice to somebody who knows more than you do and has been doing it for a long time, and who is familiar with the equipment and with the experiment. It's one of the roles of being a graduate student, for example, in advanced sciences: learning how to do experiments. Often this continues in postdoctoral fellowships. Now that's not true of all science, but it's true of a great deal of it, and the practice is complicated in developed branches of science. (Interview, 1 April 2009)

Suppes is here remarking on the centrality of apprenticeship for many scientific fields and how the practice of experimenting is learnt through a long and continuous training. This training cannot be replaced by theoretical instructions, or even those that are contained in a manual.

> Certainly you wouldn't let someone who just walked in from the street, or even a very smart fellow student or faculty member in the Department of English, walk into the room and start fiddling with the dials of equipment that involved high energy and radiation. That would be foolish nonsense. And you wouldn't hand him a manual to read to learn what to do. You'd say that he has to be taught, meaning to have a good apprenticeship before he's equipped to do this. The more complicated and expensive the equipment, the more strictly that regime is established. As I've already remarked, the manuals for equipment are usually pretty scanty. They cover a lot of important points and are very useful, but not scientifically really thorough, and above all they themselves are not written in any set-theoretical fashion ever, even though they often have a rather formal English style. What is really important is that apprenticeship, and it's ridiculous to think that the practice of what it takes to do an experiment, not to know but to do an experiment, will be formulated in a set-theoretical way, just as we don't have a set-theoretical formulation of how to play tennis or hit a golf ball or shoot a basketball or play any other sport you might name. (Interview, 1 April 2009)

Another important point Suppes makes here is that studies on education have not been much focussed so far on learning how to do things, rather than learning concepts, and even when studies have been devoted to the subject, they have been mainly concentrated on learning very specialized things, while, according to Suppes, comprehension of how people learn to perform elementary motion activities is also needed.

> Now, that practice is a part that's continually receiving more attention in philosophy of science, and it's possible also to study regimes of apprenticeship. I do think that there is a kind of gap, in that what has been done, in the study of experiments, hasn't really focused on this apprenticeship. And the kind of learning that takes place in apprenticeships is not the kind of learning that, for example, educational psychologists have primarily studied. There are exceptions to that; there are special domains in educational psychology. But a student can earn a doctorate in educational psychology and not have a single course in anything in-

volving doing things being studied as a phenomenon of learning. So what you mainly learn in educational psychology is very specialized doing, like reading—how to read. But we don't think of that in the same way as learning how to ride a bicycle or do a simple experiment. You do learn in school how to do mathematics, but it's very specialized, very cognitive. What is neglected are the practical matters of complicated physical maneuvers, the kind of things you need to get into your fingertips to do properly. Another example is learning to drive carefully. You can't just hop into your car, having read the manual, and be ready to go down the freeway. The same is true of stepping into a laboratory. If I were to make a criticism of the literature, it's the lack of study, both conceptually and in the actual detail of the learning that is involved in apprenticeships for students and others learning how to do experiments. (Interview, 1 April 2009)

This focus of Suppes' comments is particularly important, since apprenticeship in experimental practices is one of the fields where the connection between theoretical formulation and practice is neglected.

It is crucial to distinguish between experimental procedures and experimental results. When one builds empirical structures or models of data, one is usually interested in experimental results. Nonetheless, having a well-founded theory of the methodologies used to gather these results would be more than desirable and, unfortunately, is nearly totally absent from the literature in epistemology. The reasons for this absence are many and they range from the technicalities involved in most of the experimental practices to the intrinsic features of the activity of experimentation, that are for sure closer to a 'know-how' than to a 'know-that'.

This know-how is acquired through long processes of apprenticeship, like in sports. As Suppes put it in an interview:

No one reads a manual on how to ride a bicycle. Or to play tennis, as we have agreed. Good instruction has to be vague. You cannot describe the quantitative aspects of having a good tennis stroke—that is hopeless. You cannot begin to understand in detail what gets learned in complex coordination of the sensory system, the peripheral nervous system, the muscles and the neurons in the brain. Neither the best tennis player in the world, the best physiologist, nor the best neuroscientist, could describe exactly what is going on. It is a wonderful show, much too delicate, subtle, and refined for anyone to describe accurately. That is the way it is with good experimentation. How to do things, not how to think about them. (Interview, 31 March 2009)

Another serious problem is that, since these experimental practices tend to become more and more specialized as a discipline becomes more mature, it is not the case that they are acquired once and for all; if the apprenticeship is not continued (for instance, if it is abandoned for some time due to lack of funds), scientists have to be trained again and it can take time to come back to previously reached levels of know-how. An example cited by Suppes is that of brain experiments on octopuses: the fact that nowadays very few scholars work with these animals is going to mean a loss in the ability to make such experiments, despite the very high levels reached in the period ranging from the 30's to the 60's.

Another probably unavoidable problem is the poor mutual understanding between theoreticians and experimenters.

> One thing that has not been studied by philosophers very well is how such experimenters often operate without really understanding what the theoreticians are doing, but still operate very well on an experimental level. (Interview, 31 March 2009)

Again, the explanation is probably to be found in the 'learning by practice' attitude of the experimenters, but the cultural distance between theoreticians and experimenters makes it very hard to establish a methodological discourse to connect theory and experiments. As a matter of fact, maybe the most significant example of such a connection are experiments—like those of social psychologists—that are designed to show the incorrectness of someone else's theory.

There are also specific cases in which it is particularly hard to define a theory of experimentation, namely when indirect observations are involved. When you cannot directly observe a phenomenon, there are a series of decisions that you must take: what to observe, how to interpret the observation of a related phenomenon as telling something about the phenomenon you cannot observe, what counts as an experiment, etc. All these questions make it especially difficult to design a precise experimental methodology. An example of this kind of problems are experiments conducted at the beginning of the 20th century on atomic particles, whose existence could only be indirectly observed.

Nowadays, brain researches have similarly to deal with the problem of indirect observability:

What is now important about the brain is that we can learn a lot by experiments which, in their methodology, are guided by earlier experiments in psychology. The subject is responding behaviorally, by verbally saying yes or no, by some gesture or by an observable choice. In the brain, it is not so simple. We have to observe the brain's subtle activity, and then try to reason about it. (Interview, 31 March 2009)

In other terms, even if certain activities of the brain can be experimentally observed, in order to make sense of them and to connect them with cognitive processes, other kinds of experiments must be done in association with the latter, experiments in which the overt behavior of human subjects is observed. This strategy is conceptually not very different from that of scientists like Ernest Rutherford, who built a model of the atom based on the observation of the deviation of alpha rays projected on a screen after the interposition of a gold foil between the source of the rays and the screen.

This similarity is highlighted by Suppes himself:

In other cases, like observing atoms, it was hard to get to the point of observing, and then it was hard to know what we were observing. It is the same now with the brain. (Interview, 31 March 2009)

To come back to the distinction between experimental procedures and results, even though in most disciplines what is lacking is a design of the experimental procedures, psychology marks an important exception; a long tradition has consolidated a solid methodology of experimentation, but sometimes what is not really clear is how to handle the results of the experiments:

But clear ideas lie behind the experimental designs. I think what is missing is how to think about the potential results of experiments, rather than just the methodology of their design. The problem is to think of good experiments to show certain theoretical ideas are wrong. That would be the right title, rather than just the theory of designing experiments. There is a clear parallel here to mathematical thinking. Such experiments are like mathematical counterexamples. (Interview, 31 March 2009)

These features make experimental practices hardly expressible in a unitary scientific discourse. That is to say, not only the methodologies adopted in the experimental practices vary a lot from discipline to discipline, but also the explanatory discourse that integrates the results of experiments follows diverse lines of argumentation, according to the different approaches to experimental design.

Suppes states that the model-theoretic apparatus by itself is insufficient when dealing with scientific domains in which huge amounts of data come into play and the adoption of statistical techniques becomes mandatory:

> The relation between empirical structure and theory is not model-theoretic but statistical, although the statistical aspects are often not explicitly set forth in testing physical theory. (Suppes 1988a, 30)

A theory of experimentation has the purpose of describing in rigorous terms experimental procedures; these involve many different aspects: how to collect data, how to decide which, among all the recordings of the experiment, should be excluded as too anomalous and which have to be counted as data, how to connect data with the fundamental theories. The latter connection is bidirectional: from the one side, the theory shapes the data in a particular way, from the other side, a process of abstraction from the amount of data takes place; in mature disciplines, most of the times, if not always, this process is based on statistical methods. We will now enter into the details of experimental and statistical design.

5.1.2 Theory of experimental design

The role of a theory of experimentation in science is prominent; it is only through such a theory that it is possible to connect fundamental theories and the correspondent raw experimental data. For this reason, a serious theory of experimentation should find its place in any well developed scientific discipline.

The experimental methodology must depict a hierarchy of theories that are used to test the theoretical model (Suppes 1967, 63–64). This hierarchy reflects successive levels of data reduction, starting from the very beginning, from experimental reporting, which is often incomplete and strongly based on a sort of principle of authority applied to the experimenters (Suppes 1997).

The point of having a hierarchy is that, when one compares theory and experiments, one has to compare models of a different logical type (very often one has continuous functions in the model of the theory, while data have a strongly finitistic character). Suppes' way out (Suppes 1962) consists of taking into account possible realizations of data and possible realizations of a theory being tested by those very same experimental data; the latter amounts to define possible realizations of experimental procedures. Possible realizations are logically defined in the same way. The result is then a hierarchy of models, that proceeds by successive steps of abstraction.

As early as 1962, Suppes begins (Suppes 1962) to get interested in building a formal framework able to constitute a foundation for the successive analysis of experimental data. A remarkable thing here is Suppes' conviction that the theory of experimental design is not something which is only relevant for the applied side of science, detached from the original theoretical work; already when working on theory and models, one has to take into consideration experimental methodology. This is something he explicitly affirmed in a personal correspondence with Fred Suppe of 1987:

> The models of data paper was an effort to show how much more is involved and what a high level of abstraction is required already at the level of data before any statistical analysis is appropriate. I also [tried] to bring out how issues of experimental design enter already...at an abstract level at the formulation of models. (Suppe 1989)

Experimental design amounts to finding alternative hypotheses explaining a certain phenomenon or alternative methods to achieve a certain result and settling on a suitable test in order to establish which, among the alternatives, is the most efficient in terms of explanatory power or positive results.

Even if tests were widely used already in the 12th century in China, the elaboration of definite theories of testing is certainly an acquisition of the 20th century (Suppes 1974a, 7). One example of testing of a theory is its extension to a new domain: the experimenter should expect the theory not to apply to any domain whatsoever. Thus, if the results of the experiment are congruent with the theory in this extended domain, the experimenter becomes skeptical with respect to the theory (Suppes 1960).

While this need of testing is less pressing in disciplines already well developed from a theoretical standpoint, in disciplines that are strongly based on empirical results, it is fundamental to have theoretical instruments to control experimentation. In particular, in some branches of some social sciences, like psychology or sociology, the largest part of the work amounts to testing statistical hypotheses, i.e. hypotheses that can be said to (sometimes unexpectedly) emerge from data, much more than from previously thought theoretical statements driving the collection of such data. These testing instruments mainly come from a theory of experimental design or, more precisely, from a theory of statistical design; for this reason, in such disciplines the theory of experimental design must be particularly precise and detailed and it constitutes the most technical part of the discipline (Suppes 2007a).

There is an important distinction to be made here, that Suppes states in very clear terms, that between testing a theory and testing an hypothesis.

[...]

> what distinction we can draw between testing hypotheses—particularly statistically—and testing theories. Well, of course one is of much greater simplicity, usually. A hypothesis deals with a very restricted phenomenon. A theory, particularly a deep one, has a more or less endless variety of applications. This is an important distinction. For example, in testing a theory, there is all this classical discussion—which is right, even though it's hard to quantify—that in testing a theory it's better to have a great variety of experiments of different kinds to confirm a theory. In testing a hypothesis, that's not often the case. The hypothesis is stated so narrowly that the phenomena to which it applies are not very extensive. (Interview, 1 April 2009)

A relevant difference is given by the possibility (or impossibility) of being submitted to statistical testing.

> I think it's hard to draw a strict logical distinction between hypothesis and theory, but there is an informal, working one which is important. A hypothesis is a mini-theory, a tiny theory, not meant to have much range. But there's something important about that. The way statistics is done in a modern mathematical sense, hypotheses are stated in a very formal, rigorous way. But that means they're stated for a very formal, restricted case, for which the language is mathematically precise and the range of applications is equally precise, and you can't ordinarily do that with a theory. I can't take, say, Newtonian physics, and write a tight hypothesis, and have a null-hypothesis that makes any sense. So that's an important distinction, that we formalize immediately, not a formalization in the sense of formal language, but a formalization in the sense of standard mathematics. We use these formal methods easily and readily in all kinds of statistical situations. We don't have a ready method that we think is realistic for formalizing in the same kind of standard math-

ematical language in the test of a theory, statistically. We would write hypotheses that we thought were derived from the theory, and those would be formulated in precise, informal mathematical language, and then tested with appropriate experiments, where the null-hypothesis would be that the theory was true, and if we don't like choosing a null-hypothesis, then we would maybe work out the details in terms of Bayesian priors and posteriors. But in any case it would again be a statistical test in formalized and ordinary mathematical language. We wouldn't attempt that with a theory. I think that's probably the most important kind of distinction. There might be some more scholastic distinctions, but not in working practice. (Interview, 1 April 2009)

Statistical design, even if mainly used in experimental works, is a genuinely theoretical component of science (Suppes 1974a, 6). In statistical design the most important questions concern the estimation of the parameters to be used and the testing of hypotheses. In order to deal with this kind of issues it is certainly more straightforward to consider models as mathematical entities rather than physical, hence the usefulness of analyzing their set-theoretical properties (Suppes 1960). This means that when an empirical theory is given a precise formalization in set theory, it is possible to analyze its models in an innovative way, previously thought to be exclusively applicable to pure mathematics; this new way of enquiry is particularly interesting when statistics and probability come into play. The parameters, which are usually thought of as something emerging in a 'bottom up' fashion from the empirical work are then represented using a typically 'top-down' framework, namely that of mathematical models.

The set-theoretical model is at one extreme of the hierarchy connecting the fundamental theory to data; in between there are all those empirical models that represent successive levels of abstraction:

> To define formally a model as a set-theoretical entity which is a certain kind of ordered tuple consisting of a set of objects and relations and operations on these objects is not to rule out the physical model of the kind which is appealing to physicists, for the physical model may be simply taken to define the set of objects in the set-theoretical model. (Suppes 1960, 290–291)

Statistical design must also be accompanied by statistical tests; when a theory correlates two phenomena with a causal relation, one should test whether data possess some features that are called 'Markovian' (Suppes 2007a). To put it very simply, the test concerns the dependence of future states only on present states and current forces, and not on past states preceding the present one. What has also to be tested is the independence of the probability of future states from the number of trials and the fitness of observed probabilities to the predicted ones.

It is important to notice that a theory of experimental design presupposes a good theory of the disciplines for which the experiments are designed, since the latter helps in organizing the experience in a certain way and it is exactly on the basis of the experience so organized that tests and experiments are to be designed.

> In all cases where theory has been successful in science I think we can make an excellent argument for the deeper organization of experience the theory has thereby provided. A powerful theory changes our perspective on what is important and what is superficial. (Suppes 1974a, 4)

In applied sciences it is very important to have a strong interaction between the fundamental and the applied part of the discipline; this interaction results in an enrichment for both sides; thus, the role of scholars working in applied science is not only that of testing the soundness of theories elsewhere developed, but also that of proposing new theories themselves (Suppes 1974a).

Without a theory, nothing can be inferred from empirical facts, nor can predictions be made; only when these facts are organized according to a theory is it possible to have guidance in building further experiments. This is the main criticism that Suppes addresses to what he calls 'bare empiricism', to which he opposes his 'probabilistic empiricism':

> At its most extreme level, bare empiricism is simply the recording of individual facts, and with no apparatus of generalization or theory, these bare facts duly recorded lead nowhere. They do not provide even a practical guide for future experience or policy. They do not provide methods of prediction or analysis. In short, bare empiricism does not generalize. (Suppes 1974a, 6)

But there is also the other side of the coin: data. As already mentioned, data are not a direct product of an observation; they are mediated in many ways: first, especially in disciplines in which they are acquired and measured with the help of complicated instrumentation. Suppes highlighted these considerations in his reply to the paper by Ryszard Wójcicki:

It is a long way from running around the laboratory doing one thing and then another, to having a set of data as printout or on a computer screen ready for analysis. That process still needs much more thorough attention than it has received. Much of the current interest in the philosophy of science in discussing experiments has shied away from the gruesome details of exactly how data are purified and selected for analysis, not to speak of how they are generated, which itself may involve, as equipment becomes increasingly complicated, many different independent tests of reliability and accuracy of the equipment. (Wójcicki 1994, 148–149)

Suppes explicitly mentions the necessity of having, as part of a modern theory of experimental design, a precise theory of instrumentation. The main reason for having such a theory is that the equipment used for experiments is becoming more and more complicated as science advances, in some cases it is very expensive or even dangerous, so we need the experimenters to be well trained in the use of the instrumentation, and we also need to have very precise and codified procedures on the use and maintenance of these instruments.

It is necessary to have a lot of hands-on training in what it really means to run a complicated experiment with complicated instrumentation. In many cases, as in physics where there are often dangerous levels of energy involved, it is really important. Occasionally serious mistakes are made and somebody gets hurt. (Interview, 31 March 2009)

In a sense, there has been a turn from a perspective according to which instrumentation was only 'accidentally' part of the experiments and thus was each time built *ad hoc* for each experiment, towards a more professional conception of the theory of instrumentation, where instruments become the core of a specific scientific discipline.

It used to be that instrumentation was mainly built by the scientists doing the experiment; but now there is a real theory of instrumentation. The main embodiment of that, for practical purposes, crystallized, based on a lot of investigation and fundamental knowledge from past science, will be embodied in the manual given by the manufacturer, describing the functions of the equipment and also listing, of course, its limitations.

[…]

Of course there are experiments without much instrumentation, but lots of important experiments, including those on the brain and in physics generally, really depend upon the use of complex and subtle instruments. (Interview, 31 March 2009)

And the importance of having a theory of instrumentation as a part of a theory of experiment grows as scientists are making use of more and more complicated equipment. Once again, one of the examples Suppes most likes is that of studies on the brain, where complex equipment is used in the experimentation, such as electroencephalography:

> I'm looking here at a technical manual, just as an example for us, of the new EEG (electroencephalographic) unit we recently acquired. It has 128 sensors, and it is a beautiful piece of equipment. It is an extension of the old system we had, which was much smaller. Here are typical headings that you want to read about. You certainly want to read about safety; when working with anything electrical it's very important to be so concerned. A mundane but very important subject here: rinsing and disinfecting. A subject in an experiment wears a cap with the sensors on it; it is very important that you disinfect it in going from one subject to the next. Another problem is that of connectivity: examining and observing on the computer screen how the sensors are performing, which means looking at data on the flow of current. If current flow is not right, only noise will be observed. You have to have a sophisticated regime for observing these matters, and use your hands in making adjustments in fitting the cap on the subject's head when things are not working well. (Interview, 31 March 2009)

So, safety, use, and maintenance of the experimental apparatus must be considered core elements of the theory of experiment and of the scientific enterprise as a whole.

5.1.3   Theories of error

Turning now to a different but connected subject, it is worth noting that, most of the times, not all that is observed is acquired as a datum: the results of experiments are filtered and selected, in order to prune out anomalies, like those due to errors of the experimenter.

It is important to remark that in Suppes' opinion, a very important *desideratum* of any mature scientific theory is the inclusion of a serious theory of error, that should then become a central subject matter of analysis for philosophers of science. This is because in contemporary science errors cannot be reduced to 'malfunctioning' of the experimental apparatus, but they are intrinsically involved in the scientific activity, even if it is a naive attitude to think it is possible to avoid them by and large. Unfortunately, this does not usually characterize either sciences' or philosophy of science's current practice.

> The theory of error is something that is historically missing, not only from philosophy in terms of systematic working out of a theory of it, but also in science. For example, the first really detailed theories of error are as late as the latter half of the 19th century. There are hints in the *Principia* of Newton, for example, but not a systematic set of ideas. Laplace, especially, did have systematic ideas; certainly the work of Simpson, earlier in the 18th century, was also important. Notice now what I'm referring to is a combination of things: error, and thinking about the normal or Gaussian distribution depending on your field—Gaussian if you're a physicist, normal if you're a statistician. That derivation depends on the relative frequency of small errors. (Interview, 1 April 2009)

A very central point, when trying to build a theory of error, is to understand, once a certain (large enough) amount of data has been collected, which—among the measurements that considerably deviate from the others—have to be considered genuine errors. In other terms, given the unstable character of the world we live in, how can we distinguish a strange result due, for instance, to a wrong execution of experimental procedures from a correct, though unusual, measurement? Here is what Suppes has to say on the subject:

> Now, an important thing to begin with about the theory of error, particularly when we talk about it in relation to physical theories—is it really error, or is it due to variations in the environment, or small interactions with the environment? The notion of error seems to be an intentional one, as if someone were trying to do X and didn't quite do X, but did something close to X and created an error. In actual fact, the theory of error, which historically discriminates between systematic and random errors, is already making this distinction without using this terminology. "Systematic", of course, does itself sound like an intentional notion, and it is usually so. There are famous cases where observers showed some consistent bias in making observations which we refer to as systematic error. Random error occurs when we don't have an external cause we clearly identify as the source of the error. They are thought of as fluctuations in the environment, especially in the quantum world. But let's talk here as if we're just talking about the theory of errors, although I don't mind mentioning this non-intentional notion of natural fluctuations. Either one—errors that are deviations from the purest intentions, so to speak, and natural fluctuations—cause a lot of havoc in theories that are stated too precisely. (Interview, 1 April 2009)

It is crucial to distinguish between errors caused by mistaken behaviors of the experimenters, like the wrong use of experimental equipment, or a theory formulated under some sort of bias—and this is what Suppes calls 'systematic error'—and deviations from the mean values of some measurements due to the intrinsic nature of the phenomenal world, namely its being non-deterministic—and this Suppes calls 'random error'.

And in fact this distinction was completely ignored as long as science used only deterministic theories:

> For example, classical deterministic theories in the 19th century, and the beautiful developments of 19th century mathematical physics, were mainly stated in determinist form, and there was no place for either errors or natural fluctuations in the environment where the experiment was being conducted, or in the phenomena being observed. Now, it came to be realized, coming to the fore in the 20th century, that we couldn't think about these things at all without really serious consideration of error. So that now, as I've mentioned several places, it's recognized in all kinds of scientific publications that you need to say something about the error in your observations. It's very standard, for example, in astronomy, to give a very careful account, as well as in physics, but in other sciences as well. (Interview, 1 April 2009)

These remarks on errors, their nature and how theories try to accommodate them drive Suppes to a sort of classification of scientific theories.

Such classification is based on the interplay between theory and data and on the centrality of error in such interplay: whether it is systematic or random (through the reference to deterministic vs. probabilistic theories) and whether it is explicitly considered in the theory or not (through the corrigibility or incorrigibility of data).

In fact, the corrigibility of data is a very important feature of a theory, in Suppes' opinion; in a famous paper (Suppes 1974b), he sketches a preliminary taxonomy of theories based on two main properties, one intrinsic to the theories, namely its being deterministic or not, and the other inherent to the applicability of the theory to data, the latter being corrigible or incorrigible. The taxonomy thus distinguishes four kinds of theories:

- *deterministic theories with incorrigible data,* like the theory of biological parenthood in human beings, theories of fundamental measurement, and the Ptolemaic astronomy, which are deterministic as they do not involve any use of probabilistic notions and whose data are incorrigible because no theory of error is required, as if the data are assumed to exactly fit the theory;

- *deterministic theories with corrigible data*, like classical mechanics, which, even though it does not explicitly include a theory of error in its formulation, is applied to data whose exactness is questioned; if it is admitted that errors can be present in data, the issue of how to correct data arises;

- *probabilistic theories with incorrigible data*, like linear-learning theory, in which, even though the theory itself is based on statistical methods, it is assumed that data are measured and recorded exactly; usually the exactness of data is not challenged because of the simplicity of the experiments;

- *probabilistic theories with corrigible data*, like quantum mechanics, which uses a statistical apparatus both in the theory and in the treatment of errors in the data.

The centrality of the probabilistic attitude towards scientific fields that become more and more permeated with indeterminism should by now be clear. Let us see how this probabilistic attitude translates for Suppes into a philosophical stance.

5.2   Indeterminism and probability

In this section we move from the criticism that Suppes addresses against the trend in the philosophy of science, still anchored to an old deterministic image of science. According to Suppes, there is a strong need of tackling contemporary sciences, that are deeply imbued with indeterminism and make a wide use of mathematical probability.

The use of probability is not without consequences from a philosophical point of view: for instance, a new idea of rationality emerges, which is no more based on the principle of maximal utility, but rather on the capability of finding justified procedures. This shift is determined by the fact that uncertainty enters the picture of science but, interestingly, Suppes is not only concerned with fallibility of human knowledge as the source of uncertainty, but also with an intrinsically indeterministic nature of physical phenomena.

To conclude, if natural phenomena are intrinsically indeterministic, it makes no more sense to talk about causation in explanatory terms: if phenomena are not deterministically linked, we cannot explain the occurrence of an event as a result of the occurrence of another (causing) event. If we accept, with Suppes, that phenomena are just probabilistically related, we can only use this relation as a means of prediction of the occurrence of an event given the prior occurrence of the (probabilistically related) other event. This latter, predictive, notion of causality is the only one which is compatible with indeterministic and probabilistic scientific frameworks as the ones that constitute advanced science nowadays.

5.2.1 Probabilistic empiricism

In Suppes' view, the entire enterprise of analyzing science is permeated with probability. He defines his own approach as 'probabilistic empiricism', as opposed to the well known 'logical empiricism', to point out how the element of uncertainty is intrinsic when dealing with experiments and measurements, thus bringing into play the element of probability. An important aspect of probabilistic empiricism is that the methodologies used to relate models of the experiment and model of the theory are formulated in statistical terms.

Though the importance of probabilities in experimental works is widely recognized, Suppes makes here another point: what has been mostly neglected, especially by philosophers of science, is the use of probabilistic concepts already in the theories of many 19th century developments of various disciplines, in particular in biology, genetics and the social sciences (Suppes 2007a, 490).

This neglect is in part due to a naive conception of the world that permeates philosophy even nowadays:

> It is a way of thinking about the world that demands two general characteristics of its theories and its evidence. First, the theories should be absolute; the causal analysis given in the theories should be finite and ultimate. Second, the data of the experiments should rest ultimately on something that is perceptually certain and without any component of error. (Suppes 1974b, 281–282)

Probabilistic empiricism is particularly put forward by Suppes in the analysis of the social sciences, like economics and decision theory, and also learning theory, where he shows that when probability enters the picture, new ideas of rationality emerge. He distinguishes between a *kinematic* approach to rationality, according to which choices are driven by the principle of maximal utility and a *dynamic* approach, which holds that rationality lies in justified procedures to accomplish a goal. Despite this distinction, a commonality of these two approaches is that individual and subjective attitudes, especially intuition, play a key role, thus depicting an unusual sketch of rationality.

A particularly significant application of probabilistic empiricism is to be found in Suppes' approach to psychology. As well-explained in Arrighi (2006), in those works he shows his faithfulness to empiricism by subscribing to a new form of behaviorism (that has in fact been called by many 'neo-behaviorism'), where the manifest behavior[23] (like responses to stimuli) is considered central to the analysis, as the sole available form of evidence. Nonetheless, the novelty of his approach with respect to the stimulus-response models of the past consists in that he does not deny the role of internal structures in the functioning of the brain. And in fact, in recent works on brain experiments he tries to infer information about the internal processes and representations of the brain by looking for invariances in the recording of encephalographic waves (with EEG methods) generated.

Very briefly,[24] these experiments consist in presenting a series of stimuli relative to a 'unit of sense' (for instance a word, a phoneme, or a sentence) to the same subject (individual) or to different subjects. The stimuli are presented under various forms, that range from visual images, to visual representations as writings on a screen, to auditory ones, like a sound coming from a loudspeaker. Every time a stimulus is presented to a subject, the brain wave is recorded; these recordings are then split in two classes that are both averaged, from the first one a prototype is created, from the second a test wave. At this point, the subject (or subjects) is presented with random stimuli to test whether the brain waves so produced match the previously recorded waves according to the classification (so match when the random stimulus is connected with the prototype, no match otherwise).

Again, the collected data are somewhat messy and a probabilistic treatment is in Suppes' view the most appropriate, especially in those works in which he adopts a connectionist perspective (for instance, (Suppes and Liang 1998)). His insistence on the different notion of rationality that these studies let emerge is well summarized by the witty

---

[23]Interestingly enough, in one of his recent papers, written with Aimée Drolet (Drolet and Suppes 2008), a notion of behavior anchored in habits and associations rather than preferences is presented.

[24]A much more accurate description of these experiments can be found in (Arrighi 2006), to which we refer.

sentence, contained in (Suppes 2003b): "[Proust] is a better guide to human computation than Turing".

Anyway, to confine probabilistic empiricism to the social sciences is anyway too restrictive, as probabilities inhere in most of contemporary science. Take for example applied sciences, like engineering mechanics; there initial conditions cannot be considered as fixed, but subject to a certain variation, which is random. The only known reasonable way to deal with randomness is to use probabilistic concepts.

The refusal to see this probabilistic character of science for many philosophers of science is anchored, according to Suppes, in a strongly rooted belief: that mature science is certain. This is no longer the case: uncertainty is at the core of science and this is exactly the reason why nowadays probability and statistics play a key role in any field of study.

> There is, fortunately, an important way of putting why there is such dependence on statistical methods. This is based upon the fact that most science rests upon a base that has historically been anathema to many philosophers. The base on which the science rests is itself uncertain. [...] The new work, the new concepts, the new efforts, always lead initially, and, often for a long time, to uncertain results. It is, I claim, only by an understanding of probability and statistics that a philosopher of science can come to appreciate, in any sort of sophisticated way, the nature of uncertainty that is at the heart of contemporary science. (Suppes 2007a, 495)

Further, it is worth noting that Suppes believes that thinking in probabilistic terms is an attitude that crosses the boundaries of science and steps into the ordinary life of people, for instance when pragmatically evaluating the best decision to take, probabilistic concepts come into the picture.

> It is part of my theme that it is a return to realism—realism in the sense of belief and not in the sense of ontological realism—to recognize how schematic any of our knowledge of the universe must be and that it is the character of commonsense knowledge itself to be schematic and probabilistic. (Suppes 1980b, 175)

Given the uncertainty intrinsic to commonsense and scientific knowledge, Suppes would recommend a 'probabilistic turn' even in moral and economic theories, that are still not equipped to face uncertainty:

Both classical moral theory and classical economic theory ignore almost entirely the difficult and subtle problems of making rational decisions in the face of uncertainty. (Suppes 1980b, 178)

Even more interestingly, Suppes anticipates a revolution in the philosophy of mind and in the cognitive sciences and psychology that, in his opinion, will take place when a probabilistic approach will be adopted also in these disciplines.

The strong claim is that, since our mental and psychological activity comes as a flux, it is questionable whether it is possible to isolate a single behavior and interpret it as a more or less rational response deterministically caused by a stimulus of a certain kind. Once we accept that stimuli are a random flux of phenomena to which our perceptual apparatus is exposed and that such apparatus is prone to errors, it is straightforward to see how a probabilistic approach enhanced with a theory of error can result as an appropriate means to improve the study of mental and psychological activity.

From all these ideas a new conception of rationality emerges, one for which the evaluation of the rationality of a judgment or a behavior cannot be made in isolation, but has to be taken against the whole flux of mental information, extracting a sort of average value.

The flux of our internal mental machinery and the flux of the stimuli outside our minds had best be thought of in random terms, and it is only the global averaging reflected in our talk or our actions that properly should be regarded as rational. Rationality is a concept like temperature: It has no meaning when pushed downward to too small a scale of phenomena. (Suppes 1980a, 189)

So far, the use of probability in science and in commonsense thinking has been advocated, based on the uncertain character of human knowledge. In a sense, it is our ignorance of the deepest laws of nature that forces us to reason in probabilistic terms. Suppes (1980b) questions also the latter assumption while talking about radioactive decay:

There is no body of systematic evidence that a deterministic law holds, and it seems appropriate to interpret the large number of studies of these matters as directly supporting the thesis that randomness is in nature, and not simply in our ignorance of true causes as Laplace would have wanted it [...] or, to put it in more colloquial language, that the world is full of random happenings. (Suppes 1980b, 174)

Thus, while many philosophical accounts of probabilities, especially in the past, but in part also at present, considered probabilistic approaches as approximate representations of a world ruled by exact and deterministic laws, and thus eventually replaceable by non probabilistic theories as soon as science evolves, Suppes suggests that it is worth considering that natural laws could be intrinsically anchored in randomness. As Suppes notes in the reply to the commentary by Hilary Putnam to (Suppes 1974b) contained in (Suppe 1977):

> The placing of randomness, whether entirely in the observer or also in nature, continues to be of fundamental philosophical importance. (Suppe 1977, 295)

And which side of the fence is Suppes on is easy to understand by reading his illuminating book *Probabilistic Metaphysics* (Suppes 1984), whose Chapter 2 is titled "Randomness in Nature". There Suppes attempts a definition of randomness in contraposition to determinism:

> [...] phenomena are random that are not deterministic. Formulated in a somewhat more satisfactory way, we would say that such phenomena have a random component if they are not deterministic. (Suppes 1984, 30)

Determinism had been previously defined in the chapter this way:

> The intuitive notion is that phenomena are deterministic when their past uniquely determines their future. (Suppes 1984, 12)

Moreover, in that chapter Suppes provides a series of examples that show the inadequacy of a deterministic treatment and the intrinsic random nature of the described phenomena.

The clearest and most thorough manifestations of randomness in nature are, according to Suppes, radioactive decay and, more generally, quantum mechanics. In those cases the search for hidden variables that would explain such phenomena in deterministic causal terms has been predominant. Despite the plethora of scientific works dedicated to this aim, the search has always been unsuccessful and in the 1960's Bell has given an empirical demonstration of their impossibility. In the presence of continuous physical quantities, there are so many interacting causes that determine such qualities, that it is impossible to calculate their exact values. Moreover, as Heisenberg demonstrated with his principle of uncertainty, it is impossible to simultaneously measure with exactness two distinct but related physical quantities, like position and momentum. Such impossibility has nothing to do with technological limitations in the equipment currently used, but it is intrinsically impossible (Suppes 1997).

But Suppes gives other examples which are closer to our everyday experience that are evidently not prone to be deterministically accounted for, like human vision and smell.

These and other examples lead Suppes to conclude that:

> It is not just the quantum world that has an essential random component—it is almost every aspect of experience. The evidence supports the thesis that random or probabilistic phenomena are found in nature and not simply in our lack of knowledge. (Suppes 1984, 29)

Obviously, Suppes does not hold that natural phenomena are completely random: this would lead us to think that a deep understanding would be a nearly hopeless enterprise. There are always some constraints that limit the complexity of reality:

> [...] there are causal constraints that are not sufficient to determine fully the phenomena, but that can lead to fruitful causal analysis [...]. (Suppes 1984, 13)

Causal constraints are not something which is exactly determinable, they are kinds of recurrent patterns in the manifestation of phenomena to which the analysis can be anchored. So, even though science would never reach the goal of being an exact description of reality, still the sense of its endeavor can be found in the discovery of the meaning of such recurrent links.

5.2.2 Probabilistic causation

Once the intrinsically undeterministic character of nature is recognized, what happens to the notion of causality? If we know that it is not possible to single out the ultimate genuine cause of an event due to the uncertainty of natural phenomena, is it still possible to connect in some way happenings in the world? Once again, Suppes' answer comes from his probabilistic approach: causality can be expressed in probabilistic terms.[25]

---

[25]This subsection is sketchy in many respects. Although we deemed it necessary to include it in the book for the sake of completeness, nonetheless many interesting aspects have not been deeply addressed as, on the one hand, this is the part of Suppes' work which has received more attention by the philosophical community and, on the other hand, it has been extensively systematized by Suppes himself, especially in his book *Probabilistic Metaphysics* (Suppes 1984).

A field in which the use of probabilistic causation is more wide-spread is that of the social sciences and in (Suppes 1982), especially dedicated to causation in those disciplines, Suppes shows how we can build a notion of cause based on probabilistic concepts.

To put it very simply, Suppes moves from a notion of *prima facie* cause, taken from statistics, where this is expressed as a correlation between random variables, i.e. a dependency relation between two variables is established if the probability distribution shows by comparison that the two present themselves more often as correlated than separately.

The second step of the process consists in verifying whether this correlation is spurious, and this is done by introducing a third variable which is held constant and by observing whether the correlation remains or vanishes; in the latter case the correlation is said to be spurious.

At this point Suppes can give a definition of genuine cause:

> We define a prima facie cause as *genuine* cause (relative to a given framework of concepts) if and only if it is not spurious. Notice that the definition of genuine must be relativized to a framework of concepts. There is no metaphysically or scientifically ultimate concept of genuine cause. (Suppes 1982, 242)

It is worth underlining the second part of the definition, in which a very important philosophical position is contained: with uncertainty and indeterminism, we cannot have a notion of ultimate genuine cause. The notion of genuine cause is intrinsically relative and contextual. Even in this case, every talk about causality has to be conducted inside the boundaries of a theory. Only by starting from theoretical assumptions can we try to hypothesize correlations and then analyze them.

An important consequence of this characterization is that the nature of causality is no more explicative, but rather predictive. The greatest import of the discovery of a causal link is not that of explaining the intimate and ultimate connection between two phenomena, but rather that, having discovered this connection, we are able to predict what will happen when similar phenomena will present them again to our attention.

Here an orthogonal issue arises: the theory provides the frame of reference inside which to study correlations, but first of all the correlations must be hypothesized; in other words, some prior probabilities have to be put under the focus of attention. How do these priors form?

This is a very relevant question, since priors are also what informs experiments and what guides the design of the experiments. Suppes' claim is that these priors are formed by associative mechanisms, as happens in many other aspects of the formation of our knowledge and skills. In a sense, their formation doesn't differ that much from any other learning mechanism typical of human beings and other animals.

The associative mechanisms produce the expectations with respect to what will become associated to our experience. To be more precise, based on previous experience, we expect many objects and processes to come always together; Suppes has called this 'small-scale holism'. This sort of holism creates the background which is necessary for us to notice things that attract our attention and that then we inquire:

> As already mentioned, the fundamental law of perception, and the corresponding brain activity in man or animal, is contrast and change. This is what is salient. But this contrast and change require a background, in fact, an extensive background of holistic expectations that are nearly constant and also extreme in probability. (Suppes 2007b, 456)

The philosophically interesting point here is that again Suppes shows his pluralism which emerges in a mixture of theoretically different assumptions used to explain different parts of the same problem and the consequent different methodologies applied to different phases of the study of a single phenomenon. If correlations from which causality emerges are studied within a probabilistic framework, the assumption that we use as a starting point of the enquiry comes from a very different source, which is our natural learning mechanisms:

> [...] the Bayesian distribution that reflects the beliefs of the policymaker or the experimenter prior to actual experimentation for the purposes of policy or truth gathering—has not itself been obtained by what statisticians or economists would regard as rational methods. It has been obtained by the methods of learning built into organisms genetically and from experience—biological, cultural or otherwise. (Suppes 2007b, 468)

Finally, it is interesting to underline the direct link Suppes sees between experiments and causality. In his opinion, the greatest part of experiments in science are conducted with the aim of isolating causal connections among phenomena. Here is what he writes in his reply to Maria Carla Galavotti's paper:

> I emphasize of course it is possible to do experiments that do not directly bear on causality. Kinematical experiments in physics are common and in other subjects as well, but still the great bulk of experimentation is aimed at causal questions. This means that the theory of experimentation is itself an important part of the theory of causality. (Galavotti 1994, 264)

But, as we have now remarked many times, the acknowledgment of the indeterminism intrinsic in nature has led Suppes to hold a philosophical attitude that he himself has labelled as probabilistic empiricism and a theory of causation which is characterized in probabilistic terms. As a consequence, a new notion of experiment arises, close to the definition given by Kolmogorov, where probability, once again, plays a prominent role:

> We define an *experiment*, relative to the sample space X, as any partition of X, i.e., any collection of subsets of X, such that (i) the collection is a subset of the algebra $\mathfrak{F}$ of sets, (ii) the intersection of any two distinct sets in the collection is empty, and (iii) the union of the collection is X itself. This definition of an experiment originates, as far as I know, with Kolmogorov (1933). Notice that this is a technical concept within probability theory and is not meant to capture many of the nuances of meaning implied in the general scientific use of the term. Nonetheless, it is easy to give examples to show that the technical notion defined here corresponds to many of our intuitive ideas about experiments. (Suppes 1970, 107)

6

Epilogue: Determinism, Invariance and Kant Revisited

This whole book is a long-lasting and lively conversation with a great philosopher about his own philosophy.

During the interviews Suppes has repeatedly come back to his sources of inspiration and to the debt he owes to many great philosophers of the past. Thus, we deemed that the best way to conclude the book is just to metaphorically listen to the imaginary conversation between Suppes and one of his masters of the past, and one of the most influential, Immanuel Kant. So we dedicate these last pages to Suppes' re-interpretation of some of Kant's most important concepts in light of the new developments of science, in a continued comparison with some strong points Suppes himself has made throughout his works.

One of the most significant results of Suppes' attitude is the great insight gained in philosophy (not only philosophy of science, but also more traditional philosophical inquiry) thanks to his reflections on the nature of science. A beautiful example in this sense is given in this long quotation on how to look at Kant's antinomies from the perspective one assumes once errors enter into the picture of scientific thought:

> The philosophically important thing about this discussion is that it provides a way of dissolving certain paradoxes or conflicts of reason, as Kant called them. Let's consider the conflicts of reason that Kant introduces under the form of the antinomy of reason, in the second part of the transcendental dialectic of the *Critique of Pure Reason*. Now, not everyone will have read this, but the conflicts or antinomies are well known. Let's consider the first three here. The first deals with whether the time or space of the world is finite or infinite, the second with

whether matter is ultimately continuous or discrete, and the third with causality: are causes deterministic ultimately, or is there a place for absolute spontaneity? Let's take the second one, where the discussion of error is the clearest. If we have fundamental error in physics, so that the errors of measurement are bounded away from zero, then it is easy to show that we may not be able to distinguish between matter being continuous or discrete. Notice, of course, that we could discriminate the case of matter being discrete. If the pure objects of matter are large enough, then we could show discreteness, that there is not continuity. But it's the argument for continuity that remains transcendental, in the sense that we cannot offer absolutely conclusive arguments, empirically, to show that matter is continuous, as opposed to having an extraordinarily fine discreteness, this discreteness corresponding to what I call here "error." That's an important argument, not one thought about enough. By the way, the same argument applies – to take an example from the first antinomy – as to whether the space of the world is finite or infinite. Now, that seems like it ought to be a clear question, but empirically, it is not, and so therefore theoretically it's not. So, for example, suppose one hypothesis is that space is infinite, essentially something like a flat Euclidean space. The alternative is that it's finite, but a very large spherical space. Well, it's easy when you think about it, if the diameter of the spherical space, even though finite, is sufficiently large, no regime of observation now known to us could discriminate between the two possibilities. So we could not settle in a direct way, or by any indirect way that's currently available, the question of whether space is finite or infinite. It is again a transcendental question. It's transcendental because the inevitable fact of errors in measurement make it impossible to discriminate exactly between the finite and the infinite case, just as it does in the case of matter being continuous rather than discrete. Notice, of course, that this also casts a very skeptical eye on the whole mathematical treatment of manifolds, in space-time in physics. Those of you who know a little physics and a little mathematics recognize that continuity is not really enough for manifolds of space and time to be a background for physics, as we ordinarily like to think of them. They have much stronger smoothness conditions, for example, differentiability of all orders. So not only the first derivative of motion, say, but also the second derivative, the third derivative, etc., all exist and have finite values. Such very strong demands of smoothness are often required to prove important theorems. I won't mention those theorems now, but they're very prominent in mathematics and mathematical physics. The question is raised, what is the relevance of such theorems? I think that's a question that has interesting philosophical ramifications I cannot pursue here. There's another area of much greater interest for philosophers, who have a kind of idealized notion, often, of complete determinism – idealized utter determinism, we might call it – in discussing free will. So, for example, a compatibilist in free will is a person who believes you can have free will, even though the universe is completely determined. Well, you can see what I'm coming to here. If we think of the natural fluctuations, the natural presence of errors, in any experiments we try to do, it's evident we cannot establish complete determinism. Something more complicated is needed as an argument for the natural setting of free will than complete determinism. Moreover, complete determinism is, in the scientific realm, by and large not recognized as a feasible ideal. There may be some individual cases, but not in a general way, and not in that glorious idealized method of 19th century physics. It also contradicts 19th century philosophy, à la Kant and his resolution of the third antinomy, which holds that all forces are completely deterministic and make the motion of all physical objects deterministic. By the way, Newton had a similar doctrine, but he didn't use the word "deterministic", but "necessity", although it was the same idea. Somewhat to the surprise of many, including me, Hume also announces a doctrine of necessity that I consider one of his few fundamental mistakes. (Interview, 1 April 2009)

Still on Kant, there is another example in which Suppes shows how, by applying his methods to the analysis of the recent developments of science, new insights can be gained, that allow us to look at traditional philosophical concepts through new lenses. In the present case, some considerations about Einsteinian physics let emerge some similarities between the notion of invariance (which is at the core of Suppes' approach) and Kant's noumena.

So there isn't a complete resemblance there, but there is a rather striking one, including the introduction of invariance into physics for the first time in a really big way, by Einstein in his famous 1905 article on special relativity. It's now very widespread, and was widespread earlier in mathematics. So, let's take an example from special relativity that's really very simple. We have the notion of proper time. As a condition of interest in special relativity, you have different observers making observations that are moving at uniform velocity, so they're all inertial – so we hope – relative to one another. Now, is there an invariant of those measurements? Each one has his observations; they look at two points that are all moving by, and want to report on, say, their distance, which is called the proper time. They'll all get different answers because they're moving at different speeds, even though we're assuming they're using here the same kind of apparatus, with the same scales. But they get different results, which is clear to see. So if I pass you and we're observing a bicyclist and we're observing his speed, and you're moving relative to me at 10 mph, and the bicyclist is moving relative to me at 20 mph, we get very different observations of his motion. Well, the proper time says that this is a quantity that is invariant for all observers, who are good inertial observers using standard equipment. So that invariant is something like Kant's noumena. You don't have a standpoint and the phenomenological observations are the observations of individual observers. The invariant is like the noumena. Now I'm not pushing that as a final thing, but I think that is a distinction that can certainly go a certain distance in a very useful way, because we have a lot of things that observers differ on, and we'll construct different scenarios, etc., and when we think those are veridical phenomenological observation, it's a natural question of what the invariants are. If we want to modernize Kant, we could say this replaces his search for noumena, but that is certainly not the whole wild story by any means of Kant's noumena. Invariants are in the real world, noumena are not. (Interview, 1 April 2009)

References

Aristotle. 1907. *De Anima*. Cambridge University Press.

Arrighi, Claudia. 2006. Suppes from stimulus-response to brain waves analysis: A tale on the white knight of behaviorism. *Epistemologia* 29(2):267–290.

Arrighi, Claudia, Paola Cantù, Mauro De Zan, and Patrick Suppes, eds. 2009. *Logic and Pragmatism: Selected Essays by Giovanni Vailati*. Stanford, CA: CSLI Publications.

Balzer, Wolfgang, Carlos Ulises Moulines, and Joseph Sneed. 1987. *An Architectonic for Science. The Structuralist Program*. D. Reidel Publishing Company. Synthese Library.

Bourbaki, Nicolas. 2004. *Theory of Sets*. Springer.

Caamano, Maria and Patrick Suppes. 2009. Reflections on Vailati's pragmatism. In C. Arrighi, P. Cantù, M. D. Zan, and P. Suppes, eds., *Logic and Pragmatism: Selected Essays by Giovanni Vailati*, pages lxix–xcix. Stanford, CA: CSLI Publications.

Carnap, Rudolf. 1939. *Foundations of Logic and Mathematics*, vol. 1 of *International Encyclopedia of Unified Science*. Chicago and London: The Univesity of Chicago Press.

Drolet, Aimée and Partick Suppes. 2008. The good and the bad, the true and the false. In M. C. Galavotti, R. Scazzieri, and P. Suppes, eds., *Reasoning, Rationality, and Probability*, pages 13–35. Stanford, CA: CSLI Publications.

Frauchinger, Michael. 2008. Interview with Patrick Suppes. In W. K. E. Michael Frauchinger, ed., *Representation, Evidence, and Justification: Themes from Suppes*, pages 163–179. Frankfurt, Germany: Ontog Verlag.

Frigg, Roman. 2006. Scientific representation and the semantic view of theories. *Theoria* 55:49–65.

Galavotti, Maria Carla. 1994. Some observations on Patrick Suppes' philosophy of science. In P. W. Humphreys, ed., *Patrick Suppes: Scientific Philosopher*, vol. III, pages 245–264. Kluwer Academic Publisher.

Galavotti, Maria Carla. 2006. For an epistemology "from within". An introduction to Suppes' work. *Epistemologia* 29(2):213–222.

Hansson, Sven Ove. 2000. Formalization in philosophy. *The Bulletin of Symbolic Logic* 6(2):162–175.

Hempel, Carl G. 1965. *Aspects of Scientific Explanation and Other Essays in the Philosophy of Science*. New York: Free Press.

Hendricks, Vincent F. and John Symons, eds. 2005. *Formal Philosophy*. Automatic Press.

Humphreys, Paul W., ed. 1994. *Patrick Suppes: Scientific Philosopher*, vol. I. Kluwer Academic Publisher.

Krantz, David, R. Duncan Luce, Patrick Suppes, and Amos Tversky. 1971. *Foundations of Measurement, Vol. I: Additive and Polynomial Representations.* New York: Academic Press.

Luce, R. Duncan, David Krantz, Patrick Suppes, and Amos Tversky. 1990. *Foundations of Measurement, Vol. III: Representation, Axiomatization, and Invariance.* New York: Academic Press.

MacFarlane, John. 2000. *What Does it Mean to Say that Logic is Formal?*. Ph.D. thesis, University of Pittsburgh.

Mattingly, James. 2005. The structure of scientific theory change: Models versus privileged formulations. *Philosophy of Science* 72(3):365–389.

McKinsey, J.C.C. and Patrick Suppes. 1953. Philosophy and the axiomatic foundations of physics. In *Proceedings of the Eleventh International Congress of Philosophy*, vol. 6, pages 49–54.

Morrison, Margaret. 2007. Where have all the theories gone? *Philosophy of Science* 74(2):195–228.

Moulines, Carlos Ulises. 2006. Ontology, reduction, emergence: A general frame. *Synthese* 151(3):313–323.

Nagel, Ernest. 1939. The formation of modern conceptions of formal logic in the development of geometry. *Osiris* 7:142–224. Reprinted in E. Nagel, *Teleology Revisited*, New York, Columbia University Press, 1979, pp. 195-259.

Neurath, Otto. 1973. *Empiricism and Sociology*, chap. The Scientific Conception of the World, pages 299–318. Dordrecht: Reidel.

Novaes, Catarina Dutilh. 2006. *Formalisations après la Lettre. Studies in Medieval Logic and Semantics*. Ph.D. thesis, Leiden University.

Politis, Costantine. 1965. Limitations of formalization. *Philosophy of science* 32(3/4):356–360.

Psillos, Stathis. 2006. The structure, the whole structure, and nothing but the structure? *Philosophy of Science* 73(5):560–570.

Scott, Dana and Patrick Suppes. 1958. Foundational aspects of theories of measurement. *Journal of Symbolic Logic* 23(2):113–128.

Shields, Christopher. 2005. Aristotle's psychology. In E. N. Zalta, ed., *The Stanford Encycplopedia of Philosophy*.

Sneed, Joseph. 1971. *The Logical Structure of Mathematical Physics*. Dordrecht: Reidel.

Solomon, Miriam, ed. 2007. *Proceedings of the 2004 Biennial Meeting of The Philosophy of Science Association Part II: Symposia Papers*, vol. 73 of *Philosophy of Science*.

Stegmuller, W. 1979. *The Structuralist View of Theories: A Possible Analogue of the Bourbaki Programme in Physical Sciences*. Berlin: Springer.

Suppe, Frederick. 1977. *The Structure of Scientific Theories*. University of Illinois Press.

Suppe, Frederick. 1989. *The Semantic Conception of Theories and Scientific Realism*. Urbana, IL: University of Illinois Press.

Suppes, Patrick. 1951. A set of independent axioms for extensive quanities. *Portugaliae Mathematica* 10(4):163–172.

Suppes, Patrick. 1954. Some remarks on problems and methods in the philosophy of science. *Philosophy of Science* 21(3):242–248.

Suppes, Patrick. 1957. *Introduction to Logic*. New York: Van Nostrand. Reprinted in 1999 by Dover, New York.

Suppes, Patrick. 1960. A comparison of the meaning and uses of models in mathematics and the empirical sciences. *Synthese* 12(29):287–301.

Suppes, Patrick. 1962. Models of data. In E. Nagel, P. Suppes, and A. Tarski, eds., *Logic, Methodology, and Philosophy of Science: Proceedings of the 1960 International Congress*, pages 252–261. Stanford, CA: Stanford University Press.

Suppes, Patrick. 1965. Logics appropriate to empirical theories. In J. Addison, L. Henkin, and A. Tarski, eds., *The Theory of Models, Proceedings of the 1963 International Symposium at Berkeley*, pages 364–375. Amsterdam: North-Holland Publishing Company.

Suppes, Patrick. 1967. What is a scientific theory? In S. Morgenbesser, ed., *Philosophy of Science Today*, pages 55–67. New York: Basic Books.

Suppes, Patrick. 1968. The desirability of formalization in science. *Journal of Philosophy* 65(20):651–664.

Suppes, Patrick. 1969. Stimulus-response theory of finite automata. *Journal of Mathematical Psychology* 6:327–355.

Suppes, Patrick. 1970. *A Probabilistic Theory of Causality*. North-Holland Publishing Company.

Suppes, Patrick. 1972. On the problems of using mathematics in the development of the social sciences. In *Mathematics in the Social Sciences in Australia*, pages 3–15. Camberra: Australian Government Publishing Service.

Suppes, Patrick. 1974a. The place of theory in educational research. *Educational Researcher* 3:3–10.

Suppes, Patrick. 1974b. The structure of theories and the analysis of data. In F. Suppe, ed., *The Structure of Scientific Theories*, pages 266–283. Urbana, IL: University of Illinois Press.

Suppes, Patrick. 1979a. The role of formal methods in the philosophy of science. In P. D. Asquith and J. H. E. Kyburg, eds., *Current Research in Philosophy of Science*, pages 16–27. East Lansing, MI: Philosophy of Science Association.

Suppes, Patrick. 1979b. Self-profile. In R. J. Bogdan, ed., *Patrick Suppes*, Profiles, pages 3–56. Dordrecht, Holland: D. Reidel Publishing Company.

Suppes, Patrick. 1980a. Limitations of the axiomatic method in ancient Greek mathematical sciences. In J. Hintikka, D. Gruender, and E. Agazzi, eds., *Pisa Conference Proceedings*, vol. I, pages 197–213. Dordrecht: Reidel.

Suppes, Patrick. 1980b. Probabilistic empiricism and rationality. In R. Hilpinen, ed., *Rationality in Science*, pages 171–190. Dordrecht: Reidel.

Suppes, Patrick. 1982. Problems of causal analysis in the social sciences. *Epistemologia* 5:239–250.

Suppes, Patrick. 1984. *Probabilistic Metaphysics*. Oxford and New York: Basil Blackwell.

Suppes, Patrick. 1988a. Empirical structures. In E. Scheibe, ed., *The Role of Experience in Science, Proceedings of 1986 Conference of the Académie Internationale de Philosophie des Sciences (Bruxelles)*, pages 23–33. New York: Walter de Gruyter.

Suppes, Patrick. 1988b. Representation theory and the analysis of structure. *Philosophia Naturalis* 25:254–268.

Suppes, Patrick. 1992. Axiomatic methods in science. In M. Carvallo, ed., *Nature, Cognition, and System*, vol. II, pages 205–232. Kluwer Academic Publishers.

Suppes, Patrick. 1994. *Comments by Patrick Suppes to Joseph Sneed*, pages 213–216. Kluwer, Synthese Library.

Suppes, Patrick. 1997. A pluralistic view of science and its uncertainties. *Rivista Internazionale di Scienze Sociali* 1:3–18.

Suppes, Patrick. 1998. Pragmatism in physics. In P. Weingartner, G. Schurz, and G. Dorn, eds., *The Role of Pragmatics in Contemporary Philosophy*, pages 236–253. Vienna: Holder and Pichler and Tempsky.

Suppes, Patrick. 1999. The plurality of science. In J. McErlean, ed., *Philosophies of Science: From Foundations to Contemporary Issues*, pages 476–485. Belmont, CA: Wadsworth/Thompson Learning, reprinted from Proceedings of the Biennial Meeting of the Philosophy of Science Association, vol.2, 1978 edn.

Suppes, Patrick. 2001a. Axiomatic theories. In N. Smelser and P. Baltes, eds., *International Encyclopedia of the Social and Behavioral Sciences*, vol. II, pages 1026–1032. Oxford: Elsevier.

Suppes, Patrick. 2001b. Invariance, symmetry and meaning. *Foundations of Physics* 30(10):1569–1585.

Suppes, Patrick. 2002. *Representation and Invariance of Scientific Structures*. Stanford, CA: CSLI Publications.

Suppes, Patrick. 2003a. From theory to experiment and back again. In M. C. Galavotti, ed., *Observation and Experiment in the Natural and Social Sciences*, pages 1–41. Dorrecht: Kluwer Academic Publisher.

Suppes, Patrick. 2003b. Rationality, habits and freedom. In N. Dimitri, M. Basili, and I. Gilboa, eds., *Cognitive Processes and Economic Behavior*, pages 137–167. New York: Routledge.

Suppes, Patrick. 2005. The interview with Patrick Suppes. In V. F. Hendricks and J. Symons, eds., *Formal Philosophy*, pages 137–151. Automatic Press.

Suppes, Patrick. 2006. Intellectual autobiography 1979-2006. In *Proceedings of the workshop Representation, Invariance and Patrick Suppes*, pages 11–39. Center for the Study of Language and Information.

Suppes, Patrick. 2007a. Statistical concepts in philosophy of science. *Synthese* 154(3):485–496.

Suppes, Patrick. 2007b. Where do Bayesian priors come from? *Synthese* 156(3):441–471.

Suppes, Patrick. 2008a. Comment on French's symmetry, invariance and reference. In M. Frauchiger and W. K. Essler, eds., *Representation, Evidence, and Justification. Themes from Suppes*, Lauener Library of Analytical Philosophy, pages 157–161. Ontos Verlag.

Suppes, Patrick. 2008b. A revised agenda for philosophy of mind (and brain). In *Lauener Library of Analytical Philosophy*, pages 19–51. Frankfurt, Germany: Ontog Verlag.

Suppes, Patrick. 2011. Future development of scientific structures closer to experiments: Response to F.A. Muller. *Synthese* 183(1):115–126.

Suppes, Patrick. in press. Three kinds of meaning. In R. Schantz, ed., *Prospects for Meaning*. Berlin and New York: Walter de Gruyter Inc.

Suppes, Patrick, David Krantz, R. Duncan Luce, and Amos Tversky. 1989. *Foundations of Measurement, Vol. II: Geometrical, Threshold, and Probabilistic Representations*. New York: Academic Press.

Suppes, Patrick and L. Liang. 1998. Concept learning rates and transfer performance of several multivariate neural network models. In C. Dowling, F. Roberts, and P. Theuns, eds., *Recent Progress in Mathematical Psychology*, pages 227–252. Mahwah, New Jersey: Erlbaum Associates.

Tarski, Alfred. 1953. *Undecidable Theories*. Amsterdam: North-Holland Publishing Co.

van Fraassen, Bas. 1989. *Laws and Simmetry*. New York: Oxford University Press.

van Fraassen, Bas. 1997. Strucutre and perspective: philosophical perplexity and paradox. In M. L. Dalla Chiara, K. Doets, D. Mundici, and J. Van Benthem, eds., *Logic and Scientific Methods*, pages 511–530. Kluwer Academic Publisher.

Wójcicki, Ryszard. 1994. Theories and theoretical models. In P. Humphreys, ed., *Patrick Suppes: Scientific Philosopher*, vol. 2, pages 125–149. Dordrecht, The Netherlands: Kluwer Academic Publisher.

Index

actions, 82
antireductionism, 18
apprenticeship, 7, 113–115
Aquinas
St. Thomas, 95
Archimedes, 88
Aristotle, 16, 17, 87, 92, 95
doctrine of form and matter, 92
theory of perception, 92
assumption
ad hoc, 26
assumptions
choice of, 26
minimal, 100
axiom
abstract, 88
axiomatizability, 105
axiomatization, 23, 24, 30, 71, 84,
85, 96
of empirical sciences, 25
procedure for, 24
standard, 60
axioms
independence of, 42

behaviorism, 20
Bell
Alexander Graham, 132
Bourbaki

Nicolas, 72

calculus, 60
logical, 60, 62
Carnap
Rudolf, 44, 66, 70
causality
predictive, 134
causation
probabilistic, 133, 134
cause
genuine, 134
prima facie, 134
spurious, 134
computational method, 102
connectionism, 130
construction, 108
constructivism, 16
conventionalism, 29
correspondence rules, 60–62

data, 47
corrigibility of, 126
de Finetti
Bruno, 109
definition
creative, 34, 41
demarcation
principle, 105
Descartes